CW01514500

Wedding
Etiquette

Other books in the Penguin Pocket Series

THE AUSTRALIAN CALORIE COUNTER
THE AUSTRALIAN EASY SPELLER
AUSTRALIAN GARDENING CALENDAR
CASSEROLES FOR FAMILY AND FRIENDS
CHAIRING AND RUNNING MEETINGS
CHESS MADE EASY
CHOOSING A NAME FOR YOUR BABY
CHOOSING AUSTRALIAN WINES
THE COMPACT GUIDE TO WRITING LETTERS
FAMILY FIRST AID
GABRIEL GATÉ'S FAST PASTA
GABRIEL GATÉ'S FAVOURITE FAST RECIPES
GABRIEL GATÉ'S ONE-DISH DINNERS
GOOD FOOD FOR BABIES AND TODDLERS
HOW TO MAKE OVER 200 COCKTAILS
HOW TO PLAY MAH JONG
JULIE STAFFORD'S JUICING BOOK
JULIE STAFFORD'S FAT, FIBRE AND ENERGY COUNTER
MICROWAVE MEALS IN MINUTES
MICROWAVE TIPS AND TECHNIQUES
THE PENGUIN POCKET BOOK OF ETIQUETTE
THE PENGUIN POCKET BOOK OF QUOTATIONS
PLAYING CASINO GAMES TO WIN
THE POCKET AUSSIE FACT BOOK
THE POCKET CAKES AND PUDDINGS COOKBOOK
THE POCKET MUFFIN BOOK
THE POCKET WOK COOKBOOK
REMOVING STAINS AND OTHER HOUSEHOLD HINTS
SPEAKING IN PUBLIC
TRAINING YOUR MEMORY
USING YOUR NOODLES
YOUR NEW BABY

Wedding Etiquette

ANNE-MARIE McCARTHY

PENGUIN BOOKS

Penguin

Published by the Penguin Group
Penguin Books Australia Ltd
250 Camberwell Road,
Camberwell, Victoria 3124, Australia
Penguin Books Ltd
80 Strand, London WC2R 0RL, England
Penguin Putnam Inc.
375 Hudson Street, New York, New York 10014, USA
Penguin Books, a division of Pearson Canada
10 Alcorn Avenue, Toronto, Ontario, Canada M4V 3B2
Penguin Books (NZ) Ltd
Cnr Rosedale and Airborne Roads, Albany, Auckland, New Zealand
Penguin Books (South Africa) (Pty) Ltd
24 Sturdee Avenue, Rosebank, Johannesburg 2196, South Africa
Penguin Books India (P) Ltd
11, Community Centre, Panchsheel Park, New Delhi 110 017, India

First published by Penguin Books Australia Ltd 1992
This (revised edition) published by Penguin Books Australia Ltd 2000

10 9 8 7 6 5 4 3 2

Cover photograph by Simon Griffiths
Typeset by Midland Typesetters, Maryborough, Victoria
Printed and bound in Australia by McPherson's Printing Group, Maryborough, Victoria

National Library of Australia
Cataloguing-in-Publication data:

McCarthy, Anne-Marie, 1960– .
   Wedding etiquette.

   Rev. ed.
   ISBN 014 029365 5.

   1. Weddings - Planning. 2. Wedding etiquette. I. Title.
   (Series : Penguin pocket series).

395.22

www.penguin.com.au

Contents

INTRODUCTION   ix

1	**THE ENGAGEMENT**	**1**
	Making the announcement	1
	Choosing bridesmaids and groomsmen	5
	Parties	5
	The Ring	6
	Gifts	8

2	**LEGAL MATTERS**	**9**
	Minimum age	9
	Marrying relatives	10
	Second or subsequent marriages	10
	Legal documentation	10

3	**THE QUESTION OF WHERE**	**12**
	Which style?	12
	Religious ceremonies	14
	Civil ceremonies	22
	Ceremonies elsewhere	25
	The reception	27

4	**THE COST**	**33**
	Who pays?	34
	How much?	35

5	**THE BRIDAL PARTY**	**44**
	The attendants	45
	Ushers	48
	Parents of the bride and groom	49
	Master or Mistress of Ceremonies	49

6	**THE GUEST LIST**	**51**
	Who to invite	51
	The style of the invitation	52
	What to say	54
	Cancelling a wedding	59

7	**WHAT TO WEAR**	**61**
	Achieving the wedding dress	61
	Accessories	64
	Bridesmaids' outfits	66
	The men	68
	The parents	69
	Beauty	70

8	**PRE-WEDDING CELEBRATIONS**	**72**
	Be warned!	72
	Organising a pre-wedding function	73

9	**WEDDING GIFTS**	**77**
	'What do you need?'	77
	Delivering gifts	79
	Writing the thank-you notes	80
	Displaying gifts	81
	'Can we change it?'	81
	Gifts for the bridal party	82
	Gifts for each other	82
10	**REHEARSING THE CEREMONY**	**83**
	Order of ceremony	84
11	**THE DETAILS THAT MAKE THE DIFFERENCE**	**87**
	Stationery	88
	Flowers	89
	Alternatives to flowers	93
	Readings	94
	Music	94
	Photographs and videos	96
	The wedding cake	99
12	**THE RECEPTION**	**101**
	The receiving line	101
	The seating	102
	Formalities	103
	Taking your leave	106

13 AFTER THE WEDDING   **108**
    The wedding night   108
    The honeymoon   109
    Delaying your departure   109
    When you've gone   110
    Changing your name   111
    Updating your wills   112

Appendix 1: WEDDING TIMETABLE   113
Appendix 2: REGISTRIES OF BIRTHS, DEATHS
                 AND MARRIAGES   117
Appendix 3: MUSIC FOR THE CEREMONY   119
Appendix 4: FLORAL SUGGESTIONS   120
Appendix 5: GIFT SUGGESTIONS   128
Appendix 6: WEDDING ANNIVERSARIES   132
Appendix 7: WEDDING BOOK STARTER   133

INTRODUCTION

Congratulations! You're about to enter a new phase in your life. Friends will be eager to share your good news and your family will want to hear your plans for the future. But while you are enjoying the excitement of it all, keep your feet firmly on the ground: there is much careful planning to be done if you want your wedding day to be one that you can look back on with satisfaction and affection.

This book explains the traditions, customs and rituals that surround a wedding, and discusses departures from them. From the formal wedding to a casual celebration, *Wedding Etiquette* puts all the information at your fingertips. The book also provides information not readily found elsewhere: details of cost and how to stay within a budget; how to book a church and reception, and select your celebrant; who to invite and how to phrase invitations; how to give your wedding individuality; and how to avoid disasters. And, to give you extra help, there are the appendices, including a timetable counting down the weeks to your big day, a list of appropriate music, and a guide to flowers by colour and season.

Follow the steps outlined in this book and you are likely to have a wedding day that will run smoothly and be enjoyable for all, not least the bride and groom.

1 THE ENGAGEMENT

Congratulations – you've decided to get married! Organising a wedding is often hard work, but it can also be fun. Good planning will save you stress, and attention to detail will help the wedding to be the way you want it.

Work out a timetable (see Appendix 1), so that you know when each decision must be made. The first decisions often concern the engagement itself.

MAKING THE ANNOUNCEMENT

When is the right moment to announce an engagement? One couple had a party, surprised those present by announcing the engagement, and then asked everyone to move into the garden for the wedding! Most couples don't wait as long as this: it's more usual for them to make the announcement when they begin making wedding plans, or when they are well under way.

Traditionally the man asked the woman's father for her hand in marriage, and the giving of his consent formalised the engagement. Today it is usual as a first step for the couple to tell both sets of parents the good news.

Hatches, matches and despatches

Now you're free to break the news to family and friends. You've decided on a formal announcement as well? A notice in the **personal columns** of your daily newspaper helps the grapevine and isn't too expensive.

To put an announcement in the personal columns (or the 'hatches, matches and despatches' as they're often referred to!) a form must be filled in at your **local newsagency**. (Sometimes a form may not be available. In that case, writing the announcement on a piece of paper is acceptable.) Both of you must sign the form in the presence of the newsagent, who will then ring the notice through to the newspaper of your choice. (If one of you is unavailable to countersign the form, a parent or legal guardian can sign on your behalf, the only requirement being that both families are represented.) A quote for the cost of the notice will be given on the spot by the paper and you have to pay the newsagent cash. In 2000 the charge for an engagement notice in the major dailies ranged from $5.80 to $22.30 a line – a pretty cheap way of letting your friends know your good news!

While an engagement announcement can be made in a newspaper on any day of the week (except Sundays when personal columns are not published), **Saturday** seems to be the preferred day, with **Wednesday** running second. The personal columns usually take copy until just before the paper goes to press; so for a Saturday paper you'd need to lodge your notice by Friday evening. Perhaps you'd feel a little more comfortable allowing a few days' leeway!

To let family and friends living **overseas** and **interstate** know your good news you may consider placing an engagement notice in the relevant daily paper. Most interstate papers have offices in all capital cities; check under **'Newspapers'** in the **Yellow Pages**. If you cannot trace a local representative, someone at your daily newspaper will be able to recommend an **advertising agency** that will place a notice for you. An agency will also be able to place a notice in an overseas paper for you, or an announcement in a **rural newspaper**. The procedures are the same as those gone through when lodging a notice in a local paper; that is, you (or members of both your families) must both sign the relevant forms at the agency or in the office of the newspaper's local representative. The difference is the cost. While you will pay the same as the locals for a notice in an interstate paper, you can end up paying a couple of hundred dollars for an oveseas notice! Rural newspapers, on the other hand, tend to charge very reasonably.

The format of the notice is really up to you. The following examples, which range from the formal to the informal, may guide you. Note that the bride-to-be's name appears first since traditionally it is her parents who place the notice.

GREEN – BARNES Mr and Mrs Frank Green of Beaumaris have pleasure in announcing the engagement of their eldest daughter, Jane Elizabeth, to Thomas William Barnes, second son of Mr and Mrs Paul Barnes of Mentone.

A less formal notice, and perhaps the one most favoured today, names each parent individually and drops the middle names of the engaged couple.

> **GREEN – BARNES Alice and Frank Green of Beaumaris have pleasure in announcing the engagement of their eldest daughter, Jane, to Tom, second son of Cathy and Paul Barnes of Mentone.**

If one of your parents is dead the notice may be phrased this way.

> **The engagement is announced of Jane, eldest daughter of Alice Green of Beaumaris and the late Frank Green, to Tom, second son of Cathy and Paul Barnes of Mentone.**

If your parents are divorced, the notice may read as follows.

> **The engagement is announced of Jane, eldest daughter of Alice Green of Kew and Frank Green of Beaumaris, to Tom, second son of Cathy and Paul Barnes of Mentone.**

If both your parents are dead the announcement may be made by whoever is hosting the wedding. Or you may make the announcement yourselves.

> **Jane Green of Beaumaris and Tom Barnes of Mentone wish to announce their engagement to their friends and relatives.**

Other ways

There are other ways to spread your news. These include putting an announcement in a newsletter, designing a web-page, telephoning people, e-mailing, or making the announcement when friends and family are gathered together – but if you're thinking of the last method, make sure you're not stealing someone else's thunder!

CHOOSING BRIDESMAIDS AND GROOMSMEN

If you have decided to have bridesmaids and groomsmen (see Chapter 5) it's a good idea to ask them *before* your engagement is announced so that you can happily answer those who ask about the sort of wedding you plan to have. Your attendants will also help spread your news and make your engagement a wonderful and exciting time.

PARTIES

Many couples will have two small celebrations, perhaps a family party (or a party at which the two families can meet), and another gathering for friends. A dinner at which you make the announcement to a few friends can turn into a successful impromptu engagement celebration; or you can arrange for a mixed bag of guests to drop in on a Saturday or Sunday afternoon.

It is quite usual for someone to host a party for the newly engaged couple. Often parents will host a family or family-based party, while a gathering for your own age group may be organised by the bridal party, should you be having attendants, or by friends with whom you share the cost (see also Chapter 8).

You may wish to hold an engagement party yourselves – and it need not be expensive. If you are on a tight budget a drinks party with a small number of easy-to-make hors d'oeuvres is your best bet. Alcohol will be your biggest expense, but you may be able to ask guests to bring a bottle of wine.

If your engagement party is a larger affair you may wish to have a caterer. Most caterers charge per head (for more details see Chapter 4), and alcohol will be in addition. Make sure you know exactly what you are getting for your money, and stipulate your preferences. You may still need to provide platters, glasses and waiters.

THE RING

Having an engagement ring may be one of the pleasures of your engagement. You will find that even strangers comment on it! But if you allow yourselves to be caught up in the moment you may find yourselves paying for a ring you can ill afford. It's no use hankering for gems the size of the crown jewels if your budget doesn't allow it. Many couples forget the engagement ring and settle for a wedding ring on its own.

Traditionally the man bought the ring before he proposed marriage. Today this is uncommon; however, if your fiancé wishes to keep the cost of the ring to himself he may phone the jeweller in advance and ask for you to be shown rings only within a certain price range. A more acceptable approach may be to budget for the ring together.

A wide choice of rings is available, including second-hand or antique rings. Couples often have a ring made to their own design, and choose the wedding ring (or rings) at the same time. Deal only with **reputable jewellers**; you may find that friends or family can recommend some. Make sure that the jeweller gives you a **valuation certificate**, and consider **insuring** your rings immediately against loss or damage.

If you have a ring with mounted stones it's a good idea to have the setting checked regularly. Don't find yourself in the situation of the engaged woman who discovered at the end of a train journey that the diamond had fallen out of her ring, leaving her finger adorned by an empty casing!

Birthstones

If the choice of rings is too bewildering, one solution may be to consider your birthstone. The superstitious believe birthstones have mystical properties that benefit the wearer. A list is given below.

January   garnet (constancy)
February   amethyst (sincerity)
March   bloodstone (courage)
April   diamond (purity)
May   emerald (hope)
June   pearl or agate (good health)
July   ruby (passion)
August   sardonyx (married happiness)

September   sapphire (repentance)
October   opal (lovableness)
November   topaz (cheerfulness)
December   turquoise (unselfishness)

GIFTS

You will find many friends and relatives want to give you a gift to acknowledge your engagement. These gifts are usually smaller and more practical than wedding gifts. Keep track of who has given what and write a short, appreciative thank-you note. Do this early, before the wedding gifts start arriving.

Beginning the 'wedding book'

A good way to keep track of who has given what and when is to buy an exercise book in which you record each gift received and the name of the person who gave it, together with the date you sent the thank-you letter. By doing this the minute you receive a gift you will have fewer problems with mislaid cards – and lapses of memory! Use this 'wedding book' to record all aspects of the organisation of your wedding; you'll find it so much easier than juggling loose, easy-to-lose pieces of paper.

To help you begin your wedding book Appendix 7 includes pages for you to photocopy and paste into an exercise book or clip into a folder.

2 LEGAL MATTERS

Just in case there are difficulties, make sure that you understand
the legal requirements early – perhaps even before you
announce your engagement. These requirements are listed in
the **Federal Marriage Act** (1961) and provide guidelines for the
age at which one may marry, whom one may marry, how much
notice is required, who may officiate, and what witnesses are
required.

You are free to marry the person of your choice as long as
you are of a certain age, not closely related, and neither of you
is already married. The marriage must take place before a
person authorised by the State – a minister of religion or a civil
celebrant – and two witnesses over the age of 18. If you are
unsure about any point check with the **Registrar of Births,
Deaths and Marriages** in your capital city (see Appendix 2).

MINIMUM AGE

There are strict rules about the minimum age at which one may
marry. The youngest age at which a bride and groom can skip
to the altar without parental consent is 18. A girl of 16 or 17
needs written consent from her parents or legal guardian.
Between the ages of 14 and 16 she requires the permission of a

judge or magistrate, and will be instructed to attend pre-marriage counselling. Between the ages of 16 and 18 a boy must have a special order from a judge or magistrate and his parents' written consent. He will also be directed to attend pre-marriage counselling.

MARRYING RELATIVES

If you and your fiancé are related (however distantly) it is advisable to seek genetic counselling, particularly if you plan to have a family. The law does not allow you to marry a direct-line ancestor or descendant, namely a father, mother, daughter, son, brother, or sister (even if the sibling is adopted).

SECOND OR SUBSEQUENT MARRIAGES

If either of you has been married before and is now divorced or widowed you will be obliged to produce documents to prove it: a copy of a **decree nisi** or a **death certificate** will have to be given, in advance, to the person performing the marriage. For more information, contact the **Registrar of Births, Deaths and Marriages** in your capital city (see Appendix 2).

LEGAL DOCUMENTATION

You and your fiancé will need to present copies of your **birth certificates** (or statutory declarations stating why you are not able to produce them). You must lodge a **Notice of Intended**

Marriage form with your celebrant not more than six months and at least 30 days before the wedding. The forms are available from the Registrar of Births, Deaths and Marriages in your capital city, at churches, and from celebrants.

While you may arrange a wedding at less than one month's notice, the Registrar will have to be convinced that you have a valid reason for the haste, and evidence to support your request; for example if the reason is an illness, or if you are expecting a baby, you would need to produce a doctor's certificate.

In the weeks before the wedding another form, the **Declaration of Marriage**, must be signed by both parties to confirm that there is no valid reason for the wedding not to take place. Finally, after the marriage service, your signatures will be required on the wedding certificate, in the celebrant's record book, and on a form to be lodged with the Registrar of Births, Deaths and Marriages in your State.

For information about changing your name and updating your wills, see Chapter 13.

3 THE QUESTION OF WHERE

With every detail involved in planning a wedding, the key is to book early. There are other couples out there, and they may have their eye on your choice of venues; some reception centres, for example, are booked two years in advance. This means that you must decide, in plenty of time, what style of wedding you want, since that will determine which venues you consider.

It's also a good idea to make sure that your wishes are known to all concerned: it can be upsetting to discover that a choice you have taken for granted is resisted by your nearest and dearest! If you are not confident that people will remember what you want, write it all down.

This chapter will give you information about the numerous choices for both wedding ceremony and reception, and how you can organise it all.

WHICH STYLE?

You may have long dreamed of a traditional white wedding with all the trimmings; harboured a preference for a quiet ceremony; or leaned towards a civil marriage with the pomp and ceremony usually associated with a religious service. The choice is yours, and the decision should be made on the basis of what you both feel comfortable with and what will make the occasion meaningful. The general procedure for a church wedding (often used as a model for civil ceremonies) is given in Chapter 10, while details of various religious ceremonies are described in this chapter ('Religious ceremonies').

While most religious weddings are held in a building used for religious worship, a religious ceremony can sometimes be performed at another location (and remember that you do not necessarily need religious adherence to have a religious ceremony).

Civil marriages allow you more flexibility over location, and, with the civil celebrant's agreement, you may select a park, garden, a reception centre or its surrounds, a boat or a restaurant – or you may ask the celebrant to conduct the ceremony in your home. But before you head off to a deserted spot, take a moment to consider your guests (especially the elderly): will they be able to climb that hill, or cross that stream? Are they as prepared for that trek from sunlit precipice to city restaurant?

Your reception may take on the mood of the ceremony, with a formal service being followed by a sit-down dinner interspersed with speeches, bridal waltz and the cutting of the cake. A registry-office ceremony may be held before a celebratory cocktail party; or, you may decide on a ceremony attended only by immediate family and friends, and have a wider guest list for a formal reception afterwards.

RELIGIOUS CEREMONIES

Clearly, you will both be guided by your religious affiliations – where these are different, it's important to make a choice that is acceptable to both (and it's best to come to a general understanding about this before the engagement is announced).

Each religion has its own requirements. These may concern rules about divorce and remarriage (these rules vary even between Christian denominations), days of the year on which weddings may be held, pre-wedding procedures, essential parts of the ceremony, and so on. If your choice of religious ceremony takes you into unfamiliar ground, make early contact with the person likely to be officiating, and find out all about it, so that you can plan ahead.

Christian

If you have been divorced you should find out whether you can be married in the church of your choice; each denomination has its own rules, the application of which can vary from place to place and with individual circumstances.

The length of a Christian service may range from half an hour (an Anglican or Uniting Church ceremony without communion) to an hour and a half (full nuptial mass in the Catholic Church).

Many officiating ministers are happy for couples to take part in the planning of the wedding ceremony and will consider adaptations to the traditional text. They will often accept, for example, that a couple may prefer the focus of the ceremony to be on the love existing between them, rather than on thoughts about God. If you feel uncomfortable about some parts of the text and want to include passages of your own it is best to discuss it with the minister well in advance, preferably before the immediate pre-wedding meeting. Give a clear indication of what the marriage means to you both and how you want that expressed.

The Bible is the traditional source of suitable readings, although there are other possibilities. When choosing your music consider hymns or songs that can be sung by the congregation (include the words in the order of service – see 'Service books or programmes', Chapter 4) as well as solo numbers. (For further information about selecting readings and music see Chapter 11 and Appendix 3.)

Differences between wedding procedure in the various Christian denominations are usually slight (for a standard order of ceremony see Chapter 10). Described here is the procedure for four major denominations.

In the **Anglican Church** the marriage ceremony has not changed fundamentally for over a century, exceptions being the recent exclusion of two promises: the bride's promise to obey her husband and the groom's pledge to worship his bride with his body. The rest of the marriage rite, in modernised language, remains pretty much the same.

This denomination requires that notice of intended marriage ('banns') be posted before a wedding takes place. The residing priest will look after this. The marriage service may or may not include holy communion and without it the ceremony will take about half an hour. The ceremony includes prayers, scripture readings and hymns.

The traditional procedure is as follows. The bride is escorted to the chancel by her father, where she is met by the groom and the priest. After a welcome, the priest asks the congregation if there is any hindrance to the marriage, and the couple if they consent. The priest then asks: 'Who gives this woman to be married to this man?', upon which the bride's father takes her right hand and passes it to the priest who, in turn, passes it to the groom. The bride and groom face each other and join right hands to make their vows. The best man (who escorts the groom) gives the ring to the priest who in turn gives it to the groom to place on the finger of the bride. The ring ceremony may include the exchange of rings.

The priest declares: 'Those whom God has joined together, let no man put asunder' and then pronounces the couple married. Although not part of the marriage rite, it has become customary for the priest to ask the groom to kiss the bride. The ceremony ends with a blessing, and the marriage register is signed, either in the church or in the vestry.

To marry in the **Catholic Church** one partner must be Catholic, but it is not imperative that a non-Catholic partner be Christian. The Catholic partner must present certificates of birth, baptism and communion to the attending priest, and if the non-Catholic partner has any similar certification that should be presented too. The non-Catholic partner may be required to attend a course of instruction in the Catholic faith to gain an understanding of the vows the couple will be making, and he or she will be asked to consent to children of the marriage being raised as Catholics.

The marriage may take place on any day, except during Holy Week, the week before Easter. Many priests, however, don't like conducting weddings on a Sunday as this is their busiest day. You may choose to have just the marriage ceremony itself, which lasts about half an hour, or a nuptial mass (still an option if only one partner is a Catholic), which lasts about an hour and a half, includes communion, and places the marriage ceremony halfway through the mass. In either case, with the permission of the attending priest, you are free to consider a wide range of readings, hymns and songs, and to write your own vows.

In the Catholic ceremony the bride is not 'given away'. She is escorted to the altar by her father or guardian who presents her to the groom and takes his seat. The marriage ceremony itself begins with a greeting, a reading from the scriptures and a homily (sermon), followed by the exchange of vows. The couple promise to be true to each other in good times and in bad, in sickness and in health; and to love and honour each other all the days of their lives.

While it is customary for the couple to stand facing the altar for the ceremony, many couples are choosing to face the congregation for the exchange of their vows.

The exchange of vows is followed by the blessing of the ring (or rings). Verses from the Bible may be read by members of the wedding party or by guests. The congregation prays for the marriage of the couple in the 'prayers of petition'. The ceremony ends with a blessing.

To be married in a **Uniting Church** ceremony it is not essential for both parties to be Christian. It is usual to be married in a church, although exceptions may be made. At the first interview with the officiating minister you will be given a copy of the marriage service and asked to study it so that you can discuss it with him or her. As far as the vows are concerned, there are four versions for you to choose from.

The bride may be escorted into the church by her father, but 'giving away' is not encouraged; instead, there are various provisions for the families of the couple to take part in the ceremony. The bridal party may be seated at the front of the church for the readings and the sermon; the ceremony will also include prayers, usually includes hymns, songs and music, and may include holy communion. For the proclaiming of the marriage (or sometimes for the blessing) the minister may wrap one end of the ceremonial stole around the couple's joined hands: this symbolises the strengthening power of the love of God.

For marriage in the **Greek Orthodox Church** both partners are required to be baptised Christians. Civil marriages are not recognised and for the union to be sanctioned the couple must be married in a Greek Orthodox church. The priest will require the couple to produce baptismal and birth certificates. There is no required period of notice, and marriages can be celebrated on any day, depending only on the availability of the church.

On the wedding day the bride's father escorts her to the front of the sanctuary where the groom and his groomsmen wait. It is customary, as a sign of respect, for the groom to kiss his future father-in-law's hand as the bride is presented.

The ceremony is divided into two parts, the betrothal and the crowning. During the betrothal, the rings are blessed by the priest and then the best man exchanges them three times between the bride and groom. During the crowning, two crowns (circlets of fresh orange blossom) are blessed by the priest and placed on the heads of the couple. Again, the best man exchanges them between the bride and groom three times. The crowns symbolise a reward for a life of purity up to the day of the marriage and the couple's becoming king and queen of a dominion, their new family.

After the Gospel is read, bride and groom drink wine from the same cup, to indicate their intention to drink together from the cup of life. The priest then leads the couple and the bridal party three times around a table on which a Bible has been placed. This signifies that the couple's married life should always revolve around the word of God. There is no exchange of vows and the ceremony ends with a benediction.

Jewish

A couple wishing to be married in a synagogue, or in a Jewish ceremony, must make an appointment with the rabbi to discuss their intentions. While there is no documentary proof required, the rabbi will seek assurance that the couple are Jewish – this may merely be a matter of identifying the congregations to which they, or their parents, belong. If one partner is not Jewish, but wishes to be married under Jewish law, he or she will be required to undergo a conversion.

Sunday is the most popular day for Jewish weddings. Marriages are not permitted on a Saturday, the Sabbath. The style of the ceremony will largely depend on whether you or your partner are orthodox or liberal Jews, but the essentials are the same. You may choose to be married in a synagogue or any other location as long as the ceremony takes place under a chuppah (marriage canopy). Before the wedding you will be required to sign before witnesses a marriage covenant known as the Ketubah, which is available from the synagogue and symbolises the mutual obligations of the bride and groom.

As part of her preparation for the wedding it is customary for the bride to undergo a ritual immersion at a mikvah (bath house); and for the groom to be 'called up' to the synagogue on the Sabbath before the wedding day. The 'call-up' is attended by friends and parents of the couple, with women seated apart from the men. The bride should not be present (and, in fact, the custom is that the couple should not see each other the week before the wedding).

On the wedding day the couple fast (including no water) until the ceremony under the chuppah has been completed. It is customary for the bride and groom to be joined under the chuppah by their parents and grandparents. During the ceremony the rabbi instructs the mothers of the couple to escort the bride around the groom seven times. After the blessings have been completed, a glass is put under the groom's foot for him to crush. This is the height of the marriage ceremony and meant to remind all gathered of the destruction of the temple.

After the ceremony, the bride and groom are taken to a private room where they may eat and drink alone. This is symbolic of the consummation of the marriage.

Islamic

Traditionally the drawing up of the marriage contract (which may involve a ceremony) and the wedding banquet are the two most important occasions of the Islamic wedding. Depending on the cultural group, there may be a religious marriage ceremony between the two events, but the marriage is not consummated until after the banquet has taken place.

In some cultural groups the bride has a 'henna party', where her female relatives and friends gather for feasting and entertainment. One of the married women in the party paints the bride's nails and hands with henna, a red dye, to bring good luck.

The marriage ceremony may be held in a mosque or in the bride's home. Practices again vary with the cultural group: in some groups the bride and groom stand together for their vows (this is more usual), while in others the bride remains in another place with the female members of the congregation and is represented during the exchange of vows by a man to whom she has given her consent. The bride is expected to have her hair covered, and white garments are traditional for some cultures. There are no bridesmaids, although one of the witnesses may be a woman.

During the ceremony the Imam reads verses from the Koran and speaks about the importance of marriage. The fathers of the bride and groom are asked to give their consent to the marriage, after which the bridegroom promises to give the bride something in gold (a kind of dowry) to provide for her should the marriage go astray. After more prayers the ceremony ends. The wedding banquet may follow immediately, or be held later.

CIVIL CEREMONIES

If you don't want a religious ceremony, you can have a civil wedding, either at a registry office or at another location. (For information about costs see Chapter 4.)

Registry office

Your ceremony may be as formal or as casual as you like – you can wear traditional wedding clothes, have attendants, and play music. Some registry offices are in lovely historic buildings (for example the Royal Mint Building in Melbourne) that will lend charm to the occasion.

Most registry ceremonies include: a welcome to those attending; a short address about the significance of the occasion; an exchange of vows; a declaration that the marriage has taken place; and the signing of the register together with the presentation of the marriage certificate. The ceremony is usually expected to take between 15 and 20 minutes. If you think you will need longer it is best to find out whether there is a booking directly after yours.

You will have considerable choice in format. There are three **legal requirements**: a declaration by the celebrant that he or she is the officiating person; an explanation of the legal meaning of marriage; and an exchange of vows in the presence of the official celebrant and two adult witnesses. The wedding certificate is the documentary proof that the vows have been exchanged. Even the words 'I now pronounce you man and wife' are custom rather than a legal necessity. The vows can be varied as long as they include a pledge from the groom to the bride and vice versa. You may want to write your own text, including your vows; if this is the case discuss it in advance with your celebrant.

When considering a registry office ceremony take into account that you will probably be limited to **office hours**. Most registry offices are open six days a week (excluding Sunday and public holidays) but the hours during which marriages are performed will vary from State to State; they may extend from 8.30am to 4.30pm Monday to Thursday, and to 5pm on Friday and Saturday (the busiest day). You may need to plan your celebrations accordingly: if you find yourself limited to a morning booking you may consider a lunchtime reception, or simply leave an interval between the ceremony and the reception.

Also take into account the **seating capacity**: it is unlikely that you will be able to seat more than 40 in even the largest room of a registry office. When making the booking enquire about this, and draw up your guest list accordingly; you may settle for limiting the ceremony to immediate family and close friends, and having a bigger guest list for the reception.

Music is permitted at registry office weddings, but you will need to make your own arrangements (and restrictions on space may mean that taped music is the only alternative). Similarly, while some registry offices will provide names of **photographers** this is another item you will need to organise.

You will need to give the registry office at least one month's notice – and you can make the booking for a specific time up to six months in advance.

Civil celebrant

Marriage celebrants are licensed by the Commonwealth Government. A listing of celebrants in your State may be found at the **Registrar of Births, Deaths and Marriages** (see Appendix 2), or under **Celebrants–marriage–civil** in the **Yellow Pages**. You may find that friends and family are able to refer you to a suitable celebrant, or you may decide to meet a number of celebrants before making your choice.

Ask the celebrant to explain how he or she conducts the marriage ceremony (for the legal requirements and the basic format see 'Registry office' above) and be sure to discuss any variations you would like – there is considerable leeway, but the celebrant needs to feel comfortable with the ceremony to be performed.

CEREMONIES ELSEWHERE

Perhaps you've dreamed of marrying in your parents' garden, in a favourite park, or in an historic building or its grounds. Or perhaps the grounds of your reception venue make an attractive setting? Find out about getting permission to hold the ceremony at the place of your choice and whether the celebrant will attend (some religious ceremonies may present difficulty). Consider also the accessibility of the site for your guests, its vicinity to the reception site and, most importantly for an outdoor location, the weather. Even in the height of summer showers may fall and it is wise to have an alternative plan in case there is a sudden downpour: either ensure that there is adequate shelter near by, or have a plan for directing guests to another location.

Most parks and gardens, and all historic houses, require permits for weddings. Beach sites and national parks may have strict rules about car parking, music, and so on – check with the local council!

In the park

It is possible to be married in a public park or garden but be prepared for some restrictions. Booking procedures and costs vary; enquire from the **local council**. Most public parks are divided into lot numbers and the authority should be able to provide you with a map. Bookings cover one to two hours; but once again there may be some flexibility if there is no booking immediately following yours.

Many councils allow chairs and tables to be brought in for the ceremony, but this may mean carrying them some distance.

The authorities will allow a small amount of alcohol into the park for the purposes of a toast, but the requirement for a special permit usually rules out any larger liquid refreshment. A tape recorder, or in some cases a small ensemble, will be permitted as long as it does not disturb other people. Because it is regarded as litter, confetti is usually not permitted.

Historic houses and reception venues – or their grounds

For permission to hold a ceremony in an historic house, or in its grounds, contact the governing authority. A fee will apply. A ceremony can often be held at the reception venue, but some reception grounds are available only to couples who are holding their reception at that venue. There may also be restrictions, in all these situations, about where you may take photographs.

For information about buildings or grounds with an historical preservation order, contact the **National Trust** in your capital city.

Out of town

A beach location and hilltop may share the same problem: accessibility. There is little point in arranging a wedding on a romantic beach if you are forced to leave a number of guests in the car park because only the hardiest can tackle the sand dunes. Remember also that it may be windy enough to be uncomfortable, or for guests to be unable to hear the ceremony unless they are downwind.

If there is a distance to travel between wedding and reception venues it's a good idea to plan some light refreshments to sustain guests.

On the high seas

A wedding on a boat may sound romantic but could quickly turn into a disaster even if only a few guests suffer from seasickness! But if this is your choice, consider taking the immediate party on board (and remember to offer seasickness tablets beforehand, having checked with your doctor that they won't leave anyone drowsy!) and, once the vows have been exchanged, head back to shore to be met by the rest of your guests.

If you are set on a nautical wedding and reception you will need to consider the size of the craft, and its staffing and catering services. You may need to adapt your menu to take into account the movement at sea!

THE RECEPTION

Try to get a venue at which you feel comfortable. The possibilities include: a specialist reception house; a restaurant, hotel or motel; a private club; an art gallery; the local hall; an historic house; or your house. While it is legally possible to hold a reception in a public garden, this is usually ruled out by problems of accessibility: few hire companies are willing to cart chairs, tables, food and drink long distances.

Your choice will probably be influenced by your budget, the number of people you hope to invite, catering, and convenience of location, as well as your ideas about the style of reception you want.

Weighing up the options

If you are unsure about what you want, investigate a range of options. Don't hesitate to visit reception venues (most will be happy to give you a guided tour of the facilities), and find out approximate costs. This will clear the mind wonderfully: some will be too expensive, others too complicated, tawdry or fussy, or just not have that 'something' in terms of atmosphere. Other choices may be ruled out by the requirement that you be a member (in the case of most private clubs), or because they're already booked.

Once you have a shortlist, weigh up the advantages and disadvantages of each. The advantage, for example, of a reception hall with in-house catering is that much of the work is done for you. In addition, the price quoted should cover hire of the site, floral arrangements, in-house musicians and catering (but may exclude alcohol). The disadvantages may be the cost and the fact that you are likely to have less say over specific details such as menu, choice of musicians and the time at which the reception finishes. On the other hand the advantage of a self-catered reception is that you will decide every detail; however, the price you pay is a heavy workload – and self-catering is not necessarily cheaper!

The **National Trust** will provide you with a list of the historic houses available for receptions; the **Yellow Pages** also has a comprehensive listing of alternatives (under **Wedding reception**

venues; **Convention and conference venues**; **Function centres and organizers** and **Halls**) as well as caterers (under **Catering – functions**). **Local councils** will also help.

Many venues will require you to book well ahead and to pay a booking fee. They may also charge a fee if there is a cancellation. You may find that some charge a basic fee as well as an amount per head; you should request a full list of charges, and ask what extras are not covered by the fee.

Regardless of the style of your reception, your venue should be able to supply the following:

- a place for guests to leave coats and bags
- a table for presents
- dancing space (if required)
- instructions for seating arrangements
- a selection of alcoholic and soft drinks
- a microphone
- a cake table
- a room in which the bride can change, or repair her makeup
- toilets.

Specialist wedding venues

Wedding-reception houses can be the easiest alternative, since they know (or *should* know) what is expected. The quote should include hire of the venue, catering, and the standard requirements; but expect to pay extra for the in-house band, additional floral arrangements, and alcohol (a liquor licence should be provided). The reception house should also provide tables for cake and gifts, lighting, a sound system, and a room for the bride to change. Most venues demand that the reception be over by midnight, although in some places extra time may be arranged at additional cost.

Historic houses

Many historic houses in metropolitan areas are listed as specialist wedding-reception venues and come complete with caterers and equipment. Restored homesteads and historic buildings are a good alternative for country receptions (your local tourist office may be able to help if you are unsure of what is available). If the rooms are not big enough you can consider having a marquee in the grounds and using the house for pre-dinner cocktails.

As few country houses come equipped for a large wedding you will need to be prepared for a lot of hard work. You may also find that there are rules about what is and isn't permitted in an historic house.

Restaurant, hotel or motel

A restaurant, or a restaurant in a hotel or motel, may be the best alternative if you are planning a small wedding, if you want a particular style of food, or if you want more flexible hours. It is often the best alternative for people living in the country. But you may find that restaurants are loath to accept your booking unless you are able to take over the whole dining room.

When you are considering a restaurant take into account the layout of the room – will it be able to accommodate all guests with a clear view of the bridal table, or will some poor souls be out of sight around the corner, or tucked behind a pillar? Is there space for musicians, or for a dance floor, and will waiters be able to get the food and drink in with ease?

Is the restaurant capable of serving all guests more or less at once? Does it have a BYO licence; if not, how steep are the liquor prices? Does the price quoted per head include the cost of waiters?

A private house

Holding your reception in the privacy and familiarity of your own home can take a lot of the strain out of the wedding day itself. Guests are also likely to feel at ease in a private house. If your own house is not large enough, perhaps friends or relatives will offer theirs. Or, you may settle for a smaller guest list.

Other considerations may include the extra work involved in getting the house ready; the size of the kitchen (a lot of food and drink will need to be stored and prepared); the number of toilets; and the possibility of damage to furnishings.

If you choose to have your reception at home you may decide to do the catering yourself (the cheapest way of doing it), or to call in the professionals. The **Yellow Pages** has a long list of caterers (under **Catering – functions**) but word of mouth is probably the most reliable way of securing a satisfactory arrangement. If you are still stuck, consider enquiring at a local restaurant, gourmet food shop or cooking school. (For additional information see Chapter 4.)

A cocktail party or light buffet are good alternatives if you do not have the room for a sit-down meal, or prefer to keep the costs down. As in this case guests will be standing and will be unable to juggle a plate of food in one hand and a drink in the other, perhaps you should restrict refreshments to finger food. If you have a room with good access, set out the food on one large table. If space is limited put a number of tables around the room or ensure that your helpers circulate – and keep up the supply of table napkins.

For an at-home wedding, don't forget the cost of hiring a marquee, chairs, knives, napkins, heaters, coolers, lights – whatever you will need. Be prepared for the wide choice – do you prefer an all-white marquee, or a striped one? Clear sides or solid? Grass matting or wooden flooring? With every choice comes a different cost (see p. 37).

Most marquees are erected the day before the wedding, but as this does not allow much of a margin for error it may be a good idea to erect it a couple of days beforehand to make sure everything fits and nothing is dirty. Similarly, check that tablecloths are the correct size, plates match, and so on: hired equipment is big business, and as mistakes are easily made you will need to allow yourself plenty of time to rectify them. Keep a list of everything that arrives, and see that each item being returned after the wedding is checked off against it (see Chapter 13).

4 THE COST

While your wedding day will be one of the most exciting days of your life, it is also set to be one of the most expensive. But don't despair: the occasion need not be marred by the constant ticking of the cash register or by evident cutting of corners in the catering.

Keep in mind that excessive spending doesn't necessarily make a successful wedding. Settle your wedding budget, list *everything* you want, and then be prepared to modify your expectations if you cannot fit them to the budget. Put a ceiling on your spending and stay below it, no matter what – there's no fun in bleeding your parents white or starting your married life in debt.

There *can* be a lot of fun, however, in reducing the bill without taking the shine off the event or sacrificing your style. Opportunities include organising the catering yourself, doing the floral arrangements yourself, calling on relatives or friends to lend cars for the wedding party, or having a cocktail party rather than a sit-down function. You should in any case shop around for quotes on everything from photography to catering – remember that competition in the wedding market is fierce, and one firm undercutting another is not unknown.

WHO PAYS?

Traditionally the parents of the bride pay for the wedding. This, however, has ceased to be the norm; it is now just as common for the groom's parents to contribute, or for a couple to pay for the wedding themselves.

It's a good idea for the couple and the parents to sit down soon after the engagement has been announced and decide who will pay for what. If costs are to be split between two sets of parents or shared by the couple and the parents, the following traditional guidelines may help.

- **The bride or the bride's parents** pay for the engagement party, invitations and any newspaper notices. They also pay for the wedding dress, transport, reception and church venues, entertainment, the wedding cake, female attendants' gifts, photography, and stationery (including invitations, thank-you notes, order of service books, and place cards).

- **The groom or the groom's parents** pay for legal requirements, the engagement and wedding rings, the wedding suit, the celebrant, gifts for male attendants, flowers for the whole wedding party (including ushers, parents and grandparents), the wedding night, and the honeymoon.

- **Attendants** pay for their own outfits and any pre-wedding functions they organise for the bridal couple.

HOW MUCH?

Obviously costs vary enormously and your final bill will depend on a number of factors, including the location, the time of year (particularly, this will affect the price of flowers), what food you provide, and the type of entertainment you have. The information below will give you some idea of what you might pay for various items. Remember, however, that prices will vary from State to State, and from city to country.

Wedding outfits

These costs in particular will vary greatly, as wedding and bridesmaids' dresses can be hired, made (requiring payment for fabric and labour) or bought. Expect to pay between $350 and $1500 to hire a wedding dress, and $150–$600 to hire a bridesmaid's outfit. Suits for the groom and groomsmen can be hired for between $75 and $250.

It will cost approximately $1000 (excluding fabric) to have a wedding dress made; obviously the bill will escalate if intricate detail such as hand-sewn beading is required. Bridesmaids' dresses tend to cost less to make as they are not as elaborate. If your dress is made by a professional bridal boutique the cost can be as high as $5000. To have shoes covered to match your dresses will cost around $80–$120 (you supply the fabric).

Depending on how elaborate your veil is, and its length, expect to pay anything from $90 to $300 or more. And, once again, the cost of a headpiece will depend on what it is (see also Chapter 11).

Engagement party

You should allow approximately $20–$35 per guest for finger food at a cocktail party, and $15–$25 per head for a selection of beer, champagne and soft drink (see also p. 5).

Civil marriage

The Commonwealth fee for a civil marriage in a registry office is $105, and includes the cost of lodging a Notice of Intended Marriage (see Chapter 2), the certificate, and the celebrant's fee.

For another location a celebrant should charge around $300 (this is the recommended fee set by the Australian Federation of Civil Celebrants Inc.). Travelling expenses may also be charged if the place of the marriage is outside of the metropolitan area, or if other expenses will be incurred.

Religious ceremony

Your costs will vary with the kind of religious ceremony you have. For a church ceremony you may need to take into account an organist's fee, $100–$200; choir at $20–$40 per chorister; bellringers at $120; and a church donation (now more usual than an officiating minister's fee) of $100 upwards. These fees may need to be paid in advance or handed (usually by the best man) to the minister after the register has been signed.

Outdoor settings

A permit to hold the wedding service in a public park will cost around $100 for two hours and is payable to the relevant authority.

Reception or catering

This will be your major cost. Many reception centres or catering companies require a deposit and this should be deducted from the final bill. The least expensive alternative is a self-catered morning or afternoon tea; moving up the scale, for a cocktail party you might pay around $20 to $35 per head for hors d'oeuvres and $15 to $25 for drink; while a sit-down dinner in a city hotel is likely to range from $50 to $150 per head for food (depending on the menu) and $40 to $60 per head for a range of beer, standard quality red and white wines, and soft drinks.

Catering for a function at home might cost $40 upwards per head, with a $30 per head drinks bill. One way of reducing the drinks bill may be to supply your own alcohol – in the months before your wedding keep a lookout for special discounts at bottle shops. Many liquor stores are happy to do deals on large orders.

Hire for the at-home wedding

Some hire outlets offer package deals; others charge for each and every fork and table napkin. The following are approximate examples of charges (2000 prices) for a one-night hiring.

- **Marquees**. Available with a white roof and various combinations of striped and clear sides. The charge depends on size and whether you or the hire company erects it. Prices start at $350 (6 × 12 metres). Expect to pay extra for ceiling liner, flooring, walkways, and so on.
- **Flooring**. Dance floor (polished) around $8 per square metre; coir matting or synthetic turf around $4 per square metre.

- **Linen**. Large rectangular table cloth $15, table skirting $20, table napkin 75c.
- **Tables**. Round table (4 people) $10, round table (10 people) $12–$20, rectangular table (10 people) $10–$20, banquet table $80 upwards.
- **Chairs**. White plastic chair $3, folding padded chair $5, covered chair with ribbon $12.
- **Cutlery**. Wedding-cake knife $5.50, other cutlery 30c per piece.
- **Crockery**. White porcelain plate 60c, cup-and-saucer 80c.
- **Silverware**. Candelabra (five pronged) $10–$20.
- **Glasses**. Beer tumbler 40c, champagne flute 50c, mixed-drinks tumbler 40c, cocktail glass 70c, brandy balloon 70c, stemmed wineglass 40c.
- **Glassware**. Ashtray $1, cake stand $5.50, punch bowl and ladle $10–$15, salad bowl $3.50, sugar bowl $1, candle holder (single) 35c.
- **Cooking equipment**. Chafing dish (two trays) $40, gas barbecue $50 upwards, urn $25.
- **Heater and airconditioner**. Upwards of $50.
- **Lighting**. Fairy lights (20m) $25, Hawaiian flare $5, disco lights $80 upwards, extension leads $7, power box $7, dimmers $30.

Invitations

The cost will vary according to the quality of the paper, the choice of print, and the quantity (the more you order the cheaper each invitation becomes). The traditional invitation printed or engraved on vellum paper is considerably more expensive than buying the same paper blank, an option if you wish to write your own invitations.

Prices for printed invitations are normally quoted in lots of 5 or 10, with most stationers stipulating a minimum order. For 100 invitations (including envelopes) the price will range from $380 to $520 for raised print, with standard print being approximately $45 cheaper.

Service books or programmes

Many couples who decide to have order of service books or programmes buy covers (around $120 per 100) and photocopy their own inserts. It is expensive to get whole books printed, but if this is your choice the bill will be rated on the number of inserts (double pages). As an example, the full order of service for a nuptial mass would require 10 to 16 pages – 5 to 8 inserts.

Of course, it is not necessary even to buy covers. You can produce something inexpensive and attractive simply with photocopied sheets.

Photography

The cheapest alternative is to ask a friend or relative to do the photography; your outlay will then include the cost of film and printing and a thank-you gift for the photographer. Many professional photographers offer packages that include photography, printing, album, and a coverage of the day including home, ceremony and arrival at the reception.

Costs vary enormously, but expect to pay anything from $1000 to $7000. Leather or suede albums are priced around $120. Another alternative is to hire a freelance photographer from a local newspaper or magazine. Following is an approximate list of costs for a middle-of-the-range wedding photographer.

- budget wedding package (100 5"×7" prints in presentation album) $1000
- standard album package (140 5"×7" prints and 20 10"×10" enlargements in 24 side suede album) $1795
- deluxe digital 'coffee table' album $3000 upwards

Video
The standard professional video coverage lasts for five hours, and includes: film of the bride and her party preparing for the wedding at home; the ceremony; your choice of location for group portraits afterwards; and the reception. This will cost between $1500 (if your videographer stays until the bridal waltz) and upwards of $2000 (for coverage of the entire reception). This fee usually includes a master tape and two copies. Extra copies of the video can cost between $40 to $100 each.

Flowers
What you pay will be affected by your choice and by the season (see Appendix 4). Happily, there are ways of keeping the cost down (see Chapter 11). Items most likely to be supplied by a florist are listed below.

- **Bouquets**. A long teardrop bridal bouquet of roses or Singapore orchids surrounded by gypsophilia or fern, with a feature flower, $150–$250. Posy for the bridesmaid or flowergirl, around $85–$120.

- **Buttonhole**. A single rose or carnation, $7.50–$10.
- **Floral headpiece**. Can cost $75, depending on style.
- **Table centres** (as extras). Around $50 for a posy bowl.

Transport

This is an expense that is easy to avoid. Is your wedding venue, or your reception, easy walking distance? Can you find cars and drivers among family or friends, or ring a taxi? However, if you have always wanted to arrive in style the price will depend on the day of the week (evening-wedding time on a Saturday is the peak), the type of vehicle, where you live, and for how long the transport will be booked.

The hire time begins from the pick-up time at your home and ends at the drop-off at the reception. A deposit is often required, with the balance invariably sought on the wedding day. Some Saturday evening prices for cars (including ribbons and full chauffeur service) are listed below.

- **LTD**. First two hours $200, $80 per hour thereafter.
- **Mercedes**. First two hours $250, $100 per hour thereafter.
- **Jaguar**. First two hours $350, $100 per hour thereafter.

If you want a **horse-drawn carriage** (two horses) on a Saturday you will pay between $750 and $1000, depending on the quality of the carriage. This package includes picking up the bridal party half an hour earlier than otherwise needed (to allow time for photographs), and transport to the reception. Some carriages will hold eight people. If the distances are too great for the horses, the carriages can meet cars a short distance from the venues.

Wedding cake

To keep costs down, you can bake the cake yourselves and ask someone to ice it (perhaps a friend or family member if you're lucky). If you have it done professionally, the cost will depend on size and type. Most cake shops provide a range of styles to choose from, and it is possible to order the kind of cake that doubles as a dessert (for more details see Chapter 11). The following prices cover baking, icing and decorating a traditional fruit cake.

- **Single-tier** (to feed 70), $140–$220.
- **Two-tier** (100 people), $250–$340.
- **Three-tier** (150 people), $360–$600.

Music

A string quartet for two hours and a disc jockey for three hours will cost around $800 and a jazz duo for two hours and a disc jockey for three hours will cost around $700. A disc jockey alone will cost approximately $350 for four hours. For the cost of music at a church see 'Religious ceremony' above.

Wedding night

If you go to a hotel (see also Chapter 13) the price will depend on how expensive the hotel is and how lavish the room. You might pay $150 a night; or $295 or more for a honeymoon package of one night's accommodation in a suite with champagne on arrival, and breakfast the following morning.

Honeymoon

Clearly the sky's the limit: the cost may range from a night at a hotel or a weekend in the country to a gourmet tour of Europe. Many travel agents offer special deals for honeymooners and some larger bridal specialists work with travel agents to offer special honeymoon packages of wedding outfit and holiday, with extras like glamorous underwear and champagne.

5 THE BRIDAL PARTY

Being asked to attend a bride or groom is one of the greatest honours that a person can have bestowed on her or him. But before you ask your prospective attendants remember that the process can also be expensive, time-consuming, and quite a responsibility; attendants need to be reliable and supportive, and may require advanced diplomatic skills in moments of crisis. Family harmony may also be at stake – so think about it, and discuss your choices together. If any problems look as though they may arise, find a solution before they do! For example, if the friend you want to ask to be chief bridesmaid is strapped for cash because she has just bought a house, you could invite her to be your attendant on the proviso that you pay for her dress. There is usually a way round a problem that will please everyone – thinking things through early will help avoid any awkwardness later.

While attendants are part of Australian wedding custom, they are not essential: the law merely requires you to have two adult witnesses. Even if your wedding is otherwise traditional in style, you may prefer to have no attendants at all, or to have attendants who don't wear traditional gear. The sex of attendants is also part of tradition, but there is no reason why the groom should not have a 'best woman' and the bride a 'bridesman' or two, if that fits your situation – although their roles may of course be a little different.

Decide exactly what roles you would like for your attendants. If you are having a simple wedding and doing all the organising yourselves, your attendants or witnesses may need do little more than turn up on the day; on the other hand, you may be expecting them to dress a certain way and to carry out traditional tasks. Give them a chance to accept or decline on this basis.

While it is traditional to ask siblings to attend you, it is just as usual to ask a close friend. Many brides and grooms get round the problem by having some of each. Junior bridesmaids, flowergirls and pageboys are traditionally drawn from the ranks of relatives.

You may want to ask all your closest friends to walk with you down the aisle, but be restrained: bridal parties the size of a football team can look ridiculous, and can be a headache to organise in the weeks beforehand. Perhaps the best guides are the size of the venues (particularly the space at the altar or its equivalent) and the format of the wedding. Most couples don't go beyond two or three attendants for the bride, and a corresponding number for the groom.

THE ATTENDANTS

When choosing your attendants, don't feel it's necessary to have gender pairs: it is in fact traditional to have several bridesmaids and only a best man (a custom still practised in Britain);

unescorted flowergirls; or junior bridesmaids pairing with each other.

Don't worry too much about what your pairs will look like. Bear in mind that they will actually *be* paired for only a fraction of the day, and that it may be more important in the long term to choose people for other reasons. If you are worried about what the photographs will look like you can ask in advance for the photographer to arrange groupings that won't emphasise the 'odd couple'.

The chief bridesmaid

Traditionally the chief bridesmaid (or, if married, the matron of honour) has a major supporting role and helps the bride with choosing the wedding dress, organising pre-wedding functions (see Chapter 6), and dressing on the day. She may also:

- supervise the outfits of the other female attendants
- act as a witness (which involves signing the register)
- stand in the receiving line at the reception
- preside over the presents brought to the reception and organise their transport afterwards
- hand out slices of wedding cake
- and help the bride change into her going-away outfit.

Today a chief bridesmaid may also wish to make a speech, so discuss this possibility early on in the piece. If the speeches are too numerous, perhaps she could consider reading the telegrams with a groomsman. See also p. 103, 'Formalities'.

Other bridesmaids
The main duty of the other bridesmaids is to:
- help the chief bridesmaid
- stand in the receiving line at the reception
- and supervise the younger members of the party.

Best man and groomsmen
As well as giving the groom the necessary support and being a
good organiser, the best man should be capable of making a
reasonable speech. His responsibilities may include:
- organising the bucks' party
- getting the groom to the church or wedding venue on time
- taking charge of the wedding rings and producing them for
  the ring ceremony
- acting as witness
- standing in the receiving line at the reception with the rest
  of the bridal party
- and making a speech in response to that made by the groom.

Depending on the style of the wedding, he may have other
responsibilities, which can be shared with the groomsmen.
These include:
- collecting the wedding suits
- checking that the transport and the flowers for the bridal
  party are arriving according to plan
- paying any fees on the day
- and helping to organise groups for photographs.

Reading the telegrams is usually the role of a groomsman and should be sorted out before the wedding day. See also p. 103, 'Formalities'.

Flowergirls and pageboys

Younger members of the family may be keen to play a role in your wedding. While it is difficult to say what age is too young, child attendants should be old enough not to have a change of heart halfway down the aisle, wander off in the middle of the ceremony, insist on holding the bride's hand throughout the proceedings, or leave a puddle on the altar carpet!

If your small attendants are not immediate members of the family you must be prepared to have a parent close at hand, and to ask older attendants to look after them in between times. Very young attendants need not go to the reception, but for older ones it will be an important part of the fun – so make sure that their needs are considered.

USHERS

While ushers (traditionally male) are usually associated with the formal wedding, it is helpful to have someone to greet guests as they arrive at the wedding venue, hand out service books or programmes, direct people to their seats, and cope with any incidental organisation. Think of guests who would enjoy a special role – sisters, brothers, cousins or friends.

PARENTS OF THE BRIDE AND GROOM

The father of the bride has two traditional tasks: escorting the bride to the wedding and giving her away; and making a speech at the reception. Traditionally the mother of the bride helps her daughter on the morning of the wedding and acts as hostess at the reception; in Jewish custom the mothers of the bride and groom also take part in the ceremony (see p. 19).

Departures from traditional roles for parents can produce happy results. A bride can be escorted to the wedding by both her parents, or given away by her mother, who can likewise be asked to make a speech at the reception. You may choose to involve the groom's parents by asking one to read at the ceremony and the other to act as MC (Master or Mistress of Ceremonies).

MASTER OR MISTRESS OF CEREMONIES

If speeches are to be a feature of your reception, then the appointment of a Master or Mistress of Ceremonies is important to ensure smooth travelling from one part of the proceedings to the next.

The MC is usually a close family friend (for example your parents' oldest friend or a godparent) or a relative (a brother, an aunt, or even a parent). Because it is the job of the MC to keep things rolling smoothly during the official part of the reception it's a good idea to choose someone who won't be daunted by speaking to a crowd and who is somewhat of a natural entertainer. Remember to ask the person you wish to be MC well ahead of the event to avoid disappointment.

The role of the MC includes:

- calling for the attention of the guests
- offering a brief introduction and comment on the day
- proposing the loyal toast (if tradition is to be observed)
- introducing the first speaker, and subsequent speakers.

See also p. 103, 'Formalities'.

6 THE GUEST LIST

The number of people you wish to have at your wedding will largely determine where the ceremony and reception are held, and the cost of the day. Don't cram too many guests into a venue or go into debt merely to invite every acquaintance you and your fiancé have made in the last five years! But you should be satisfied that on your wedding day you are surrounded by family and friends.

Guest lists can be touchy affairs – most people regard being invited to a wedding as a compliment – and drawing one up requires thought. Inevitably there will be people who are disappointed when they learn they have not been invited, but most will understand the situation. One way of involving people who are not being invited to the wedding is to ask them to the engagement party or to one of the pre-wedding functions.

WHO TO INVITE

Start with a list that includes everyone you would like to invite: immediate family, essential relatives, old family friends, and friends of you and your fiancé. Your budget should give you a rough idea of how many guests you can manage without breaking the bank. Now it's time to get down to names.

Traditionally the guest list was made up in thirds, with one third being family and friends of the bride's parents, one third family and friends of the groom's parents, and the rest friends of the couple. This is a useful starting-point; however, the deciding factors may be the size of each family, the number of 'must haves', and who is paying for the day.

Even though your parents and your attendants don't need formal notice, it is a good idea to send them an invitation as a memento. There may also be people who are unlikely to attend the wedding (because they live interstate, overseas, or are too ill) but would still be pleased to receive an invitation; send invitations to these and count *most* of them out!

Be careful to take into account people who may not necessarily be on your guest list; for example the minister or celebrant (and partner), the photographer, and anyone who is helping you as a favour on the day. Remember also that some guests regarded as single may want to bring a friend – do you allow for this? It's best to make some discreet enquiries first. If there is a particular friend, put his or her name on the same invitation, for example 'Chris Rowe and Robin Davis'; if this can't be established, simply add 'and friend' after the guest's name.

THE STYLE OF THE INVITATION

The style and wording of the invitation should be in keeping with the style of your wedding: a formal affair may call for an embossed card, while a more casual wedding may simply require a handwritten note. However, there are no hard-and-fast rules; in the end it's your choice.

Newsagents have a wide range of writing paper suitable for handwritten invitations, and a stationer will give you a bewildering choice of printed styles, including coloured, cream or white paper, motifs, borders, illustrations and initials. Once again, your choice will be defined by your personal taste and your purse (for details of costs see Chapter 4). Don't, however, be persuaded into a combination of paper, type and colour that makes the invitation almost impossible to read – legibility is important!

You will need envelopes to match. Remember also that it is better to overcalculate the number of invitations needed (this applies to all wedding stationery) than to find yourself short when you decide to send additional ones. Left-overs can be kept as mementoes, even for children and grandchildren!

Once you have decided on the style of the invitation take care to handwrite rather than type guests' names. This gives your invitations a more personal air.

Sending them out

Invitations should be sent out well in advance of the wedding day, ideally at least eight weeks before the wedding – don't forget that you must allow two lots of postage time! You should in any case send invitations to interstate and overseas guests earlier than this to allow them time to make the more complicated arrangements necessary to attend the wedding.

WHAT TO SAY

Your wedding invitations should be sent out in the name of whoever is hosting your wedding; this may be yourselves, your parents (either one or both sets), a guardian, relative or friend. All invitations, formal or casual, should clearly state the date and time of the wedding; the addresses of venues for the ceremony and the reception; and RSVP date. You may also wish to include a reference to the appropriate attire. If your wedding is to be held in a location that is difficult to find, enclose a good clear map, and attach it to the invitation. If your wedding is to be in the country, or interstate or overseas people will be attending, you may like to include a note with their invitation advising them of suitable accommodation (you may, in fact, even book rooms on behalf of guests, see Appendix 1).

'Black tie' or 'Glad rags'?

Traditionally, invitations do not include dress code. Guests could once safely assume that the time of the wedding dictated the dressing requirements, as follows.

- **Morning suit.** Traditionally worn to a morning wedding and comprising grey, striped trousers, a cut-away coat, and a grey top hat in extremely formal situations. If worn at all, the morning suit is usually only worn by the bridal party and perhaps the fathers of the bride and groom.

  Women attending a wedding at which morning suits are to be worn wear a smart suit or dress and usually a hat.

- **Lounge suit**. A dark or grey suit (single or double-breasted) is worn to a daytime wedding. Women tend to wear a smart suit or dress and maybe a hat.

- **Black tie**. A dinner suit is worn to a wedding that takes place at or after 5pm. Women wear cocktail dresses or evening wear.
- **White tie**. Tails are worn to very formal evening weddings that take place after 6pm. Women often wear long evening dresses to this sort of function.

However, these rules are no longer adhered to and your guests will welcome some guidelines. Usually these are given in terms of what the *men* wear (as above); for example 'Lounge suit' on an invitation is generally understood to mean that while *men* wear suits and ties, *women* wear a smart suit or dress. 'Black tie' on an invitation means that while men wear dinner suits women wear a formal gown or a cocktail dress. Include on the invitation whatever you think will help your guests to turn up dressed for the mood of the day. 'Semi-formal', 'Lounge suit or jacket', or even 'Glad rags' may do the trick in these more relaxed times.

Reply if you please ...

RSVP dates are also not printed on the traditional wedding invitation, the assumption being that the reply should be received within seven days. But so few people would now understand this that it is advisable to give an RSVP date that will give guests two or three weeks to sort out their own arrangements, and yourselves at least four weeks to finalise all the details that depend on having firm numbers.

You may find guests are lax about replying, or that a reply goes astray. If you have not had a response by the due date you may need to ring the defaulter, or get a tactful third party to enquire for you.

Sample wording

Traditionally, a wedding invitation is worded like this if the bride's parents are hosting the wedding.

Mr and Mrs John Carew
request the pleasure of your company
at the marriage of their daughter
Elizabeth Mary
with
Charles Andrew Smith
at St Thomas's Church, Summerdale
on Saturday, 9 December 2000
at 5 pm
and afterwards at
The Meadow Grove Reception Centre
561 Albany Rd, Oceanside

58 Thanet Street   **Black tie**
Summerdale
NSW

If both parents are hosting the wedding, and you want wording that is less traditional, you might choose something like this for the first part of the invitation (if you decide against 'Mr' and 'Mrs' the woman's name is usually given first).

**Ruth and John Carew
and
Kathleen and James Smith
request the pleasure of your company
at the marriage of
Elizabeth Mary Carew and Charles Andrew Smith**

If only one of your parents is hosting the wedding, that parent's name appears alone with the appropriate changes made elsewhere.

**Mrs Barbara Shaw
requests the pleasure of your company
at the marriage of her daughter**

If your parents are divorced but are hosting the wedding together, the first part of the invitation may be worded as follows.

**Mrs Barbara Shaw and Mr John Shaw
request the pleasure of your company**

Or, if your mother has remarried, the following wording can be used.

Mrs Barbara Morgan and Mr John Shaw

However, if your mother and your stepfather are hosting the wedding the first part of the invitation will read 'Mr and Mrs Graham Morgan' and 'her daughter' will be substituted for 'their daughter'.

If you are holding the wedding yourselves, and you want phrasing that is a little less formal, the invitation may read as follows.

Clare Holmes and Paul Lane
would like to invite you
to their wedding at 11 am on 9 December 2000
at the Lily-pond Lawn, Botanic Gardens, South Sydney

A party to celebrate the occasion will be held
afterwards at
Pearson's Restaurant, 41 Rose Street, South Sydney

RSVP   **Dress informal**
Clare Holmes
5 Smith Street
Eaglesnest 2999
(Tel. 9331 3424)

An informally worded invitation can be sent as a letter.

Tel. (02) 9335 4111   **197 Dell Road**
Armidale
NSW 2350
9 October 2000

Dear Michael and Amy

We have pleasure in inviting you to the wedding of our daughter Jane to Tom Kelly. The ceremony will be at St Paul's Church, Settlement Street, Armidale at 11.30 am on 9 December 2000, and will be followed by a reception at home, 197 Dell Road, Armidale. Please reply by 9 November 2000 to the above address; or phone us if it is more convenient. Suggested dress is lounge suit or jacket.

We hope very much that you will be able to join us.

Denise and John Jones

CANCELLING A WEDDING

Obviously having to cancel a wedding is a traumatic situation for all involved, but there are matters that need to be dealt with. Arrangements must be cancelled, guests informed, and gifts returned. Although it's better to be honest with yourselves rather than to face marriage unhappily it is far simpler if you decide to call it off before the organisation is too far down the track: there is little that can be done with dress fabric that has already been cut or invitations that have been printed, and these bills will have to be paid in full, adding to the unhappiness of the situation. Even when a cancellation is made weeks in advance, reception centres, photographers and caterers are likely to demand a cancellation fee.

Letting people know

The least painful way to inform guests of the cancellation is by a short note in the mail; but if your change of plan occurs on the eve of the wedding you will have to make phone calls, send lettergrams, faxes or e-mails – anything to let guests know in time. It is not necessary to give a reason for the cancellation, and probably better if you don't, as you may find yourselves back together again with fully briefed guests still debating whether it was the right decision!

If you find it too overwhelming to contact guests personally, appoint parents, your attendants or friends to do it on your behalf. You will invariably find that people are more concerned with your happiness than with any inconvenience to their own plans.

Returning gifts

If a wedding is cancelled all gifts are returned to givers as soon as possible. If guests are being told of the change of plan by phone, arrangements can be made then.

If an engagement ring is a gift from a woman's former fiancé, it is correct for her to return it; if it has been paid for jointly, it's a matter for negotiation.

Your wedding dress and bridesmaids' outfits may be the most noticed aspect of your wedding. Even the most informal wedding calls for a sense of occasion: regardless of how casual you want the day, remember that you will all need to feel good and be satisfied afterwards that you have looked your best.

While the traditional bride walks down the aisle in flowing white, there are no hard-and-fast rules about how you dress – and there is no need to follow fashion. A full-length wedding gown is usually chosen for a formal afternoon or evening wedding, while a shorter dress or a suit may be right for a more intimate or casual celebration. You can also choose an elegant evening dress or a cocktail dress. What you wear will depend on your preference and your purse.

ACHIEVING THE WEDDING DRESS

Finding the right wedding dress can take a long time. Before actually hitting the shops, look through some bridal magazines to find out whether you like what seems to be in fashion. You will find, as well as formal dresses, short, simple styles, often worn without a veil. Don't discount other fashion magazines, especially for ideas for bridesmaids' dresses.

Think of your own wardrobe: is there a particular dress, jacket or shirt that really suits you? If there is, consider using its mood and line as a model for the kind of dress you want. Have you thought about finding an antique dress, or wearing your mother's or your grandmother's?

Once you have an idea of what you want it may be time to go to the shops. Look at fabrics, dress patterns, and dresses for hire as well as what bridal boutiques are offering. This will help you to decide whether to make your dress yourself, buy it off the rack, hire it, find a dressmaker, or have it designed and made up by a bridal boutique.

If you can, go to the evening-wear section of the big department stores. Many stores provide a wardrobe consultancy service that, though not strictly a wedding service, can offer advice on everything from dresses to shoes and accessories.

The cost of a wedding dress may vary from $350 to $6000 or more (for more details see p. 35). How much you want to spend should be settled well before you make your final decision. The fabric will be the major cost factor; satin or silk will be more expensive than a fabric like taffeta. If you have set your heart on a fabric that is expensive, see if you can find a style that uses less of it, for example a dress with a shorter, straighter skirt.

Having it made

Looking for a dressmaker? If friends cannot suggest a good, reliable one ask at fabric shops. Larger bridal boutiques often offer both a dressmaking and an off-the-rack service and will provide a comparison of costs. Make sure that you are booked in at the dressmaker's well in advance of the wedding, especially if you are getting married in spring or summer, when he or she will be at his or her busiest.

When you go to your dressmaker explain *exactly* what you want with the aid of sketches, photographs or another dress – and provide some detailed notes. Keep up a good level of communication while the dress is being made. If there's a long silence, find out what is happening; if you think the dress isn't going as planned, say so at once.

Getting it right

Horror stories of brides' dresses abound! The hem too short (because the bride didn't take along the shoes she would be wearing on the day); the hem missing altogether; the veil not the same white as the dress; even alterations still being done the night before the wedding. Make sure your outfit is not added to the list of stories. Decide on your wedding dress at least a couple of months before the wedding, especially if it is being made, to allow plenty of time to overcome problems. Try on your dress with *all* the accessories. Check the outfit in daylight as well as in artificial light.

As you may lose weight before the wedding (either by choice or through stress) have a final fitting about a week before the day, just to make sure there's no last-minute panic because your dress is too loose.

The colour

While white is customary, almost anything goes, and white doesn't suit everyone. You can choose one of the cream shades (oyster, ivory or antique). You can wear black, although Grandma may keel over at the sight of it!

If you're being married a second time, or simply don't want to wear white or cream, consider a pastel shade, or a deep colour. If your budget allows it, or if someone suggests it as a present, go to a colour and image consultant (look in the **Yellow Pages**) to find out what suits you best. You may be surprised.

ACCESSORIES

The tradition of having 'something old, something new, something borrowed, something blue' is easy to follow when you are choosing accessories.

The pieces you choose may have special significance. The 'something old' (or borrowed) is often a piece of jewellery, perhaps the pearls your mother wore for her wedding, or a brooch that was your grandmother's. Some brides wear a fancy blue garter for tossing to the single men at the end of the reception. Whatever you choose should complement your dress.

The veil

A veil may be your most important accessory if you're dressing as a traditional bride. Its style (including the headgear) will depend on the style of your dress. Once again, magazines will show long and short styles and will provide good indications of which veil suits which dress. But while veils are always popular, there are alternatives. A hat or a circlet of flowers, for example, can look equally as attractive.

Jewellery
Earrings and necklaces should be simple yet elegant. Pearls are traditional and diamonds are *always* in fashion, while gold and silver are popular. While bridesmaids don't need to wear identical jewellery, the pieces should complement each other. You may give your bridesmaids a piece of jewellery as a thank-you present that they can wear for the wedding.

Shoes
Shoes should be comfortable enough for long periods of standing: it is best to buy both yours and your bridesmaids' at least a month before the wedding so that you can break them in thoroughly. Remember that a good shoe specialist can dye your shoes or cover them with your dress fabric.

Underwear
Tried-and-true garments may be the most comfortable ones. New slips can cling and bunch, camisole straps can droop over shoulders, and strapless bras can cut cruelly: 'wear them in' beforehand. Many dressmakers recommend that a 'merry widow' is worn to achieve a firm line under a wedding dress with a fitted bodice (by all accounts it's a good piece of advice!).

The spare pair

Pantihose or stockings shouldn't be a last-minute thought. There are dozens of suitable styles, and some manufacturers have a special bridal range. Try on your pantihose just as you would any other garment for your wedding-day. Think of the bride who discovered that her only pantihose were too short; she was forced to cut the crotch out to make the pantihose fit, and spent the rest of the day listening to the tiny sounds of nylon tearing with every move she made!

Make sure you have at least two pairs on hand: nervous fingers may rip or tear them on the day.

Emergency kit

Be prepared for a last-minute repair. Assemble an emergency kit – spare buttons, needles and safety pins, thread and press studs in the right colour – and then you can relax.

BRIDESMAIDS' OUTFITS

If you thought selecting your bridesmaids was difficult, wait until you try to decide on their dresses! No two figures, or tastes, are alike. Cost should be the first consideration, as it is generally accepted that bridesmaids will pay for their own dresses. It is also worth remembering that most bridesmaids are happier to pay for something they will wear again; while your ideas may seem inspired, your brides-maids may not share your enthusiasm, especially if it means they'll be paying hundreds of dollars for a little number that will see out its days tucked at the back of the wardrobe.

The choices
Bridesmaids' dresses should complement – but never over-shadow – the bride's dress. Bridesmaids may have outfits that match, or are different in style and colour. Or they may wear short dresses or suits, happy choices if they want an outfit they can wear later. If your bridesmaids are in different styles, you can give their appearance continuity by having them wear the same accessories, perhaps matching headgear or the same jewellery.

Hire services
If the bridesmaids' budgets are tight, consider hiring dresses. Don't look only at the bridal hire stores. If you are having only one or two bridesmaids you may prefer to investigate a formal-dress hire service, which offers everything from simple cocktail wear to elegant evening dresses.

Getting a match
If your dress and the bridesmaids' are to be made, try to get them all done by the same dressmaker. If one bridesmaid lives at an impossible distance you can send fabric, patterns and sketches; however, if you can get another bridesmaid's dress made early and send that one to copy, you are likely to get a better match. In any case, make sure you send everything well in advance to allow for any changes or alterations.

THE MEN

The general tradition is for men in a bridal party to wear restrained colours and styles that will act as a foil for the more showy clothes of the women; if, however, you want the men's outfits to pick up a colour in the women's, a coloured cummerbund or tie may be the answer. Whatever is chosen, the dress of the men should complement the dress of the bride and her attendants.

Traditional choices

For a formal evening wedding either white tie or black tie is worn by the men in the bridal party. The choice for daytime weddings runs from morning dress (that is, cut-away jacket, striped pants, cravat or tie and top hat) to a classic double- or single-breasted suit worn with a shirt and tie. If you are planning an informal wedding you may prefer to wear a jacket and tie or even an open-necked shirt. See also p. 54.

Matching the details

It is best to have the men's suits matching in style and colour, but if this is not possible (perhaps the groom and the best man are wearing black double-breasted jackets, while the groomsman is wearing a black single-breasted jacket) try at least to have the shirts and ties matching.

Hiring

If it's likely to be a once-off wearing, groom and attendants usually hire their outfits. You will find that hire organisations offer a number of variations on the traditional themes.

Check the fittings several months before the wedding in case alterations need to be done. A deposit is often required and you should ask whether the cost of hire includes cleaning and insurance (in case the suit is damaged), and when the suit must be returned.

THE PARENTS

While there are specialists in outfits for **mothers** of brides and grooms, alternatives include dress shops and dressmakers.

The outfit should be in keeping with the style of the occasion. If the wedding is formal mothers may decide to wear full-length or cocktail-length dresses, while a suit may be appropriate for a daytime wedding.

The important thing is for the two mothers to communicate about their outfits in order to avoid uncomfortable differences or – worse – too much similarity. Mothers should draw a lesson from the narrow escape one pair had when they discovered (in time) that they had bought identical outfits!

Traditionally the **fathers** of the bride and groom follow the example of the men in the bridal party: if they are in morning suits, the fathers should also wear morning suits, and so on.

When the wedding day arrives, mothers are usually provided with a corsage (regarded as a gift from the groom) and fathers wear a buttonhole (for more details see p. 90).

BEAUTY

Some brides start a health and beauty programme in the weeks and months leading up to the wedding. This usually means a series of facials, pedicures and manicures. The aim, of course, is to look your glowing best for the day. The **Yellow Pages** will provide a list of beauticians, but it is probably best to go to someone recommended.

Facials
Of course you may not need or want any beauty treatment, and for the uninitiated it can be fraught with problems: a facial may be followed by an outbreak of pimples, while some hair removal can cause a rash until the skin becomes accustomed to it. If you want to have some kind of beauty 'treat' that you haven't had before, try it out well in advance, and don't in any case have a facial the day before your wedding: at least a week beforehand is safer.

Hair styles
If you are intending to use the services of a hairdresser, make an appointment before the wedding to try out styles with your headgear (the bridesmaids should do this too). Avoid anything that is radically different from your usual hair style; don't join

the army of brides who have had to see out their wedding day with a too-short haircut or an irreversibly frizzy perm.

On your wedding day it may be a great convenience to have your hairdresser come to the house. If you decide to do this, leave a good margin of time: hair that has to 'go up', for example, may need two tries, and there may be interruptions or other hitches.

Makeup

The key to successful makeup is to look as natural as possible. Some brides decide to have their makeup and nails done by a makeup artist, who will come to the house on the day of the wedding. Others feel more comfortable doing their own. Whatever you decide, you should try out various colours of lipstick or eyeshadow while you are wearing something the same colour as your wedding outfit. The bridesmaids' makeup should harmonise with yours.

8 PRE-WEDDING CELEBRATIONS

The weeks leading up to your wedding are likely to be hectic and stressful, and you may welcome the opportunity to take a break from the planning with a lunch party, a cocktail party or night out with close friends or your wedding party. Particularly if the wedding is to be a big occasion you should take the opportunity to get together with a smaller group of friends for a more intimate celebration; however, if you want the weeks or days before the wedding to stay quiet, make sure you say so, and don't be drawn into commitments that you may later regret.

BE WARNED!

Horrendous tales abound of bridegrooms showing up at the altar pasty-faced, legs in plaster and generally well under the weather after a 'bucks' night' on the town. And brides-to-be haven't been shy when it comes to celebrating the last days of their spinsterhood either! Unfortunately the dark side of the bucks' night or hens' night is not always exaggerated. But there are more restrained alternatives to a pub crawl or a night at a strip club.

Pre-wedding celebrations should be fun, but you should draw

the line at anything that is dangerous or that will lead to embarrassment or wedding-day misery. Whatever you decide, keep it simple, and schedule the party one or two weeks before the wedding to allow recovery time if events get out of hand.

ORGANISING A PRE-WEDDING FUNCTION

This may simply be a matter of a phone call from whoever is giving the party. The catering may be provided by you, shared between you and the hosts, or provided entirely by the hosts; the invitation may ask guests to 'bring a plate'; or you may call in the professionals. If you feel awkward about receiving pre-wedding gifts (particularly if guests have already been committed to engagement and wedding presents) it is best to say 'No gifts, please' on the invitation.

Engagement party

While many couples like to celebrate their engagement with a party held soon after they've made their announcement, some like to have one closer to the wedding (see also Chapter 1). Usually held by the bridal party, this function can take virtually any form and offers the couple the chance to celebrate with friends who haven't been invited to the wedding. It may be a simple barbecue, a dressy drinks party, a full-on bash – whatever you want to make it.

One popular 'theme' for a late-in-the-piece engagement party is the **cellar tea**, where guests are asked to bring a bottle to help stock the soon-to-be-wed couple's cellar.

Of course, there's no reason why you need stop at one party (except, perhaps, exhaustion!). Family and friends seem to love throwing parties once you're engaged – although difficult to do, you may need to learn to say 'no' if you think it's all getting too much.

Shower or kitchen tea

Traditionally a bride has been 'showered' with small gifts for her new home at a party given by a close relative and attended by her female friends. The presumption was that the bride had been living at home and had none of the small essentials for running a home of her own. At the shower or kitchen tea cleaning tips and recipes would be passed on by the married women.

Clearly for many brides this is an outdated concept and in Australia the more popular celebration has been a kitchen tea where friends gather to discuss the wedding day and present small gifts. These may include knick-knacks for the kitchen and bathroom, and non-perishable items for the pantry. Guests are often invited to bring a recipe too. The kitchen tea may be given by bridesmaids, a relative or friend.

There are alternatives to the shower or kitchen tea. At a linen party guests give items to stock the linen closet; for a garden party, plants and garden tools may be brought (and the party held in the garden).

Hens' and bucks' nights

The bucks' (or stags') night has long been considered the groom's final fling, a chance for him to get together with his male friends and paint the town red. Usually arranged by the best man, the **bucks' night** is often held at a hotel or nightclub. Alcohol may be high on the agenda, and it may be difficult for the bridegroom to control events if his friends are hell-bent on destruction.

If you are concerned about the possibility of a wild bucks' night, make your feelings clear from the beginning, to the best man as well as to the groom. Perhaps the groom will prefer to gather friends for a quiet dinner at a restaurant rather than have a night at a pub. But whatever is decided, it is prudent to hold the celebration well in advance of the wedding – it is most unwise for the bucks' night to be held the night before.

A fairly recent institution, the **hens' night** gives the bride an opportunity to let her hair down with her female friends. This has the same pitfalls as the bucks' night but can be fun if kept under control.

You and your fiancé may decide, however, that you can happily forgo the single-sex celebrations in favour of an occasion you can enjoy together. Particularly if you each have close friends of the opposite sex, it may be better to join the sexes in one celebration – perhaps a cocktail party, a buffet or a lunch party.

A night with the bridal party

This is an opportunity for you both to thank your attendants for their support, and to discuss the wedding in a relaxed atmosphere. It may be particularly appropriate if members of the bridal party don't know each other. The gathering may also be the time to give your attendants their gifts, especially if you have chosen something to be used or worn on the wedding day (for what to give, see p. 82).

9 WEDDING GIFTS

Receiving gifts is undoubtedly part of the pleasure of getting married and is likely to be your first concrete sign of the wedding day drawing near. While the practice of giving gifts to an engaged couple was initiated to help them establish their new home, wedding gifts are chosen more as a mark of the important occasion, and are usually larger, grander, or more enduring than engagement presents. It is assumed that persons invited to the wedding and the reception will give a present, whether they are attending or not.

'WHAT DO YOU NEED?'

You may be surprised at the number of people who want some direction about what to give; no one wants to double up or give you something that will stay in a dark cupboard for decades. And the chances are that you and your fiancé already have most ordinary household items – perhaps already in duplicate! Even if you are still living with your parents you may have collected towels, table linen and tureens to your liking.

The phone list

If you are having a small wedding, compile a list of items and leave this by your phone or split it between your mother and a bridesmaid to help guests who enquire; then as each item is suggested it should be ticked off. Tailor the list to the category of guest likely to enquire: perhaps give your mother the more expensive items that older guests and relatives may be better able to afford.

Appendix 5 lists suggestions you may like to consider adding to your list.

The bridal register

This is an efficient gift-giving system that guests can be invited to use if they wish. The service is provided by many **gifts shops, homeware and furniture stores** and by most **department stores**.

The store holds for you a multi-paged list of the stocked items that might be considered for wedding presents. Attached to this list are cover pages that detail the names of the bride and groom, the date of the wedding, the location of the reception, the address for sending gifts, and the general colour scheme for each room. Items are listed in categories (for example 'Cookware' and 'Manchester') with space for recording the brands or patterns you prefer, and the appropriate quantities.

Before the register is opened you fill in all the details and cross off anything you don't want (alternatively the list may be drawn up in consultation); after that, the store crosses off items as they are chosen, and delivers the purchases as required.

Guests can ask for the register at the store and select a gift at a price they are happy to pay, secure in the knowledge that it is an item the couple wants. The register gives guests the opportunity to contribute towards an expensive item, for example a dinner set or a cutlery set.

It is important for you to be confident that the outlet is conveniently placed, carries a good stock of the items you want, and that there is a wide price range. It may be appropriate to organise two lists (be careful not to duplicate), one at a big store and the other in a local shopping centre, to give guests a choice of where to shop.

Appendix 5 lists suggestions you may like to add to your register.

DELIVERING GIFTS

Gifts are usually delivered to the bride's home two weeks before the wedding day. The accompanying card should include the giver's address for convenience when it's time to write the thank-you notes. Fragile items should not be sent through the post.

If a present must be taken to the wedding or the reception, the parcel should be addressed to the couple. A table should be organised for presents that guests bring with them. Sadly, presents have been known to disappear from the best receptions: see that the table is placed in full view, and appoint a bridesmaid or groomsman to keep track of the parcels (they should not be opened at the reception) and to deliver them safely afterwards. This also applies to receptions held at home;

unfortunate stories about staff employed for the occasion making off with the presents are not unusual.

WRITING THE THANK-YOU NOTES

It is essential for each gift to be acknowledged (see also Chapter 1). Once the responsibility of the bride, this has become a task for both partners. It is best dealt with in an orderly fashion and should be completed within two months of the wedding – and the sooner the better. Don't rely on memory: as each gift is received, list the giver's name and details of the article; keeping a 'wedding book', as mentioned in Chapter 1, is perhaps the best way to do this. A small note indicating your pleasure at receiving the gift, and perhaps a thought about what it will mean to you, will suffice. Here is an example.

7 Lilac Street
Beechwood 5127
7 January 2001

Dear Grandma Chapman

Thank you very much for the all-purpose portable barbecue. It is far grander than anything either of us have ever cooked meat on; and we can reassure you that it works well, because we have tried it out twice already!

It was a most thoughtful present and we much appreciate it.

Love from us both

Julie and Rod

DISPLAYING GIFTS

Wedding gifts are traditionally displayed at the home of the bride's parents in the fortnight preceding the wedding day and on the day itself. In our parents' or grandparents' day this might have occasioned a grand afternoon tea party, with gifts and the bride's trousseau laid out in various rooms. Now, it is more likely that callers to the house will be invited to look at the gifts. Few will decline! Cheques should not be displayed (but you may consider writing a card stating that Mr and Mrs Smith presented a cheque).

You may both feel, however, that gift-giving is a personal matter between giver and receiver, or that for security reasons it is best not to have all the wedding presents in one house. Older traditions did not include displaying presents – so there is a precedent if you decide not to!

'CAN WE CHANGE IT?'

Too many toasters and no glasses? Perhaps a present that defies description? Don't despair: most guests are only too happy for you to swap their gifts. Similarly, most shops will be happy to accommodate you (although they may require a receipt, and expect you to choose something not less than the value of the original).

Sometimes you may need to weigh up the inconvenience of having something you don't need – or want – against the risk of hurting the giver's feelings. If the gift is from a close friend or relative you will usually feel comfortable explaining the situation and asking where the present was purchased; and some guests may make it easy by providing you with the information *and* the receipt when they deliver the present. Take early action: most shops are less willing to change an item weeks or months after the purchase date.

GIFTS FOR THE BRIDAL PARTY

It is customary for the bride and groom to give small presents to the members of their wedding party who have supported them through pre-wedding highs and lows. These gifts should be tokens rather than elaborate gestures and may include earrings for the bridesmaids and flowergirls, cuff links for the groom's attendants, photograph frames for everyone, or a different present for each attendant. The presents may be given to the wedding party when gathered before the wedding, or as the reception draws to a close.

GIFTS FOR EACH OTHER

This is purely a personal choice. Certainly giving each other wedding gifts is more a matter of inclination than tradition.

10 REHEARSING THE CEREMONY

By now you will already have decided what type of ceremony you want and who will be involved. But even the most prepared bride and groom will benefit from a rehearsal – no matter how simple the wedding. Best held a week or so before the big day, the rehearsal may vary from a run-through of procedure with the celebrant to a more detailed rehearsal in the church, led by the minister and with all the bridal party present. If you are having singers or musicians at the ceremony ask them to come too. If you are unable to arrange a rehearsal with your celebrant you can still organise a run-through of the procedure with your wedding party.

The rehearsal is the time to iron out the details of the ceremony: to decide the timing of your entry and your walk up the aisle; to check the positioning of musicians and try out the music; to sort out where the members of the wedding party should stand or sit during the ceremony; and so on. This is also the opportunity to check the lights and the sound system should you be using both or either.

While it is unlikely that a rehearsal will guarantee a faultless day, it will familiarise the wedding party with the events of the big day and help to make everyone feel more comfortable.

ORDER OF CEREMONY

While there are numerous variations, the following is 'standard' church wedding-ceremony procedure. You can use this as a model even if you are not being married in a church: ceremonies in other locations, including civil ceremonies, commonly follow this general order. For more details see Chapter 3.

- Ushers arrive 25 minutes before the appointed hour, in time to direct earliest guests to seats and to attend to any last-minute organisation.
- The groom and his attendants arrive 20 minutes before the time of the ceremony and wait in the church or the vestry.
- Musicians arrive in time to be playing as guests arrive.
- Guests arrive (15 minutes before the appointed hour) and are escorted to their seats, the bride's family and friends on the left side, the groom's on the right. The front row of seats may be reserved for the bridal party; otherwise they are kept for the parents and immediate families of the bride and groom.
- The groom and his attendants take up their positions next to the officiating minister.
- The bride's mother arrives (just before the bride) and is escorted by an usher or relative to her seat.
- The bride, her father and attendants arrive (it is courteous to be on time, and many officiating ministers will insist on it) and pause at the entrance of the church while the attendants check the bride's dress and veil and the whole party take up their positions. While it is customary for the bride to take

her father's left arm it has become just as common for the bride to take his right arm. If the bride is not escorted or given away the groom meets her at the entrance.

- The processional music begins when the bride's party is ready (a signal should be given) and the congregation stands.
- At the end of the aisle the bridesmaids move to the left, the bride stands next to the groom and her father steps back one pace (if he is giving the bride away) or returns to his pew.
- The officiating minister greets those assembled and performs the marriage ceremony, which will include vows, a ring ceremony, and a formal pronouncement that the couple are married. According to the denomination, the ceremony itself may be accompanied by (or interspersed with) hymns, songs, prayers, readings, an address, mass or communion (for more details see Chapter 3).
- The couple, minister and the witnesses sign the marriage register (either in the vestry or in the church) and the minister presents the couple with the marriage certificate.
- Recessional music is played. The bride takes the groom's right hand and walks down the aisle, followed by the wedding party, parents and the rest of the congregation.
- Photographs of the wedding party and immediate family are taken outside the church. (Don't wait any longer, as you may find it impossible to drag individuals away from friends!)
- Traditionally confetti is thrown over the couple outside the church. Be warned, though, that confetti can stain clothing and is difficult to clean up – in fact many venues ban it. Rose

petals are an older tradition and less messy. Pot-pourri or rice are also suitable substitutes.

- The bride and groom and attendants leave for the reception, perhaps making a detour to a scenic site for further photographs.

11 THE DETAILS THAT MAKE THE DIFFERENCE

As most weddings follow a similar pattern it is up to you to give your day some individuality. The difference between an ordinary wedding and a memorable one may simply be cleverly designed stationery, a church full of flowers, a band that has everyone up and dancing, or an inspired menu.

It is easy to take many important details of a wedding for granted – to assume that because you have hired an organist or a band that you will get the music you want, or to rely on a florist to come up with the perfect arrangement with no guidance from you. But the importance of planning each detail cannot be overlooked.

Itemise each major component of the wedding – the stationery, the flowers, arriving at the church, transport, music, photography, and so on – and then consider every aspect of each item. For example, write down every possible photograph you want taken from before you leave home to your departure from the reception, and all the details of the music you expect to hear throughout the day.

STATIONERY

For information about **invitations** see chapters 4 and 6.

Order of service sheets or programmes

The service sheet or programme is a good way of helping guests to participate. It may include words of readings and hymns or songs and explain who the people in the wedding party are. More modern ones may include illustrations or even a photograph. An imaginative service sheet may be valued as a memento of the occasion. (For information about cost, see p. 39.)

Place cards

These are essential for orderly seating arrangements. While the more expensive choice will be to order place cards with your initials printed on them, there is a wide range of blank cards that you can prepare yourself – and probably with more individual results, especially if you have a friend or a relative who is a dab hand at calligraphy or whose handwriting is attractive.

Menu cards

These are probably more applicable if you are providing guests with a choice of dishes or wines, but even if there is only one selection you may decide that it is a nice touch.

Cake bags

The practice of giving guests a slice of wedding cake to take home has its origins in the belief that a woman who placed the cake under her pillow would dream of the man she would marry. The slices may be put into cake bags, available at newsagents. But you can wrap them in something different, if you want a special effect; and in any case, some guests will eat theirs on the spot!

FLOWERS

Bouquets, buttonholes, corsages and crowns

While the possibilities for flowers carried or worn may at first seem overwhelming, the season will limit your choice (unless you are prepared to pay a premium for out-of-season flowers).

When making your selection keep in mind that the flowers are likely to be on display for at least seven hours and should be able to last the distance. If you are getting married in the hotter months remember that some flowers (for example white roses) wilt quickly and will brown in the heat.

A florist is your best guide (see also Appendix 4), and will also be able to give you advice about the design of bouquets and headpieces. Most florists have albums of arrangements they have done for previous weddings, and these will be a good starting-point.

Take along drawings of your bridal outfits and pieces of the fabric. Your final selection may echo the style of the wedding; roses are most appropriate for an old-fashioned wedding; while for a modern wedding you may choose flowers such as tulips or lilies.

The following guidelines may be useful.

● **Your bridal bouquet** should complement your wedding dress and be something you like. The arrangement should not dwarf you, or be so small that it is insignificant. Make sure that it's not too heavy: you will have to carry it, and if you throw it later you don't want to risk knocking a guest unconscious! Some bouquets have a small detachable posy for the throwing ritual.

- **Bridesmaids' posies** should be less elaborate than the bride's bouquet and may pick up a theme from it or draw inspiration from the dresses. The posies should match, and be easy to hold to make good photographs less of a gamble. Baskets of flowers are a possibility for flowergirls.

- The groom, male attendants, ushers and fathers of the bride and groom may wear **buttonholes**. A small flower or a bud is usual, the safest choice being a white or a cream flower, perhaps a carnation, rosebud or orchid. Or you may prefer the buttonholes of the bridal party to pick up a colour in the bridesmaids' posies, and the others to be white or cream.

- Mothers and grandmothers of the bride and groom traditionally wear **corsages**, and the choice is best made to suit respective outfits. Since corsages are sometimes disliked, consider as an alternative a small spray that can be carried or pinned to a handbag.

- **Floral headgear** may be worn as a crown, on a comb, or simply as flowers scattered in the hair. As fixing flowers to hair is fiddly and difficult you and your bridesmaids should consult the florist (ask if there's an album of brides wearing that florist's headgear) and plan a trial run with the hairdresser.

Which ones?

Certain flowers (including white roses, chrysanthemums, orchids and gypsophila) are popular choices for weddings. Other flowers, such as arum lilies (traditionally associated with death) and yellow roses (a sign of infidelity) are avoided by some. But it is up to you; your choice may be determined by your budget, the colour of the dresses and the season – or you may simply decide to have your favourites (for a list giving season and colour see Appendix 4).

At home, at the wedding venue, at the reception

Flowers will fill a room with scent and colour, create an atmosphere, and hide ugly doors, poles and walls. Early in your wedding preparations it is important to consider where and how you want flowers used. Here is a list of the possibilities for floral arrangements.

- **At home** – for photographs.
- **At the wedding venue** – altar or its equivalent, register table, pews, porch or foyer. Check whether the venue provides flowers (few do); or if there is another wedding the same day (it may be possible to share them). Flowers may be taken to the registry office; something portable, for example bouquets, may be best.
- **At the reception venue** – foyer, wedding table, table centres (if supplied they may need to be supplemented), present table, cake table.

Doing them yourself

If you have a gift for arranging flowers you may consider doing the flowers yourself. This is one way of giving your wedding individuality – floral arrangements can be predictable – but think carefully about what is involved. It may be safer to arrange the flowers for the ceremony and the reception (it's a favourite job for mothers and aunts, who may also organise flowers from their own or friends' gardens) and to leave bouquets and headpieces to the professionals.

Costing the options

Once you know what arrangements you want you should get quotes from a number of florists – and compare these with the cost of doing them yourself with flowers bought in bunches from a florist or flower market. A further possibility is to buy flowers to supplement those you can supply yourself. See p. 40 for some sample prices.

At home

If you are having your reception at home consider hiring tubs of flowering plants, growing your own, or borrowing friends' potplants. Keep table centre-pieces low so that they will not impede conversations across tables, and check that vases are stable. Vines are especially effective at hiding unsightly marquee poles. If the reception is in a marquee don't forget that the interior of the house may also need bowls of flowers.

Collecting and transporting flowers

Don't find yourself in the situation of one couple who forgot to allocate the responsibility of picking up the flowers and caused a last-minute dash through the suburbs! The collection of the flowers should be given to a responsible person (it's often a groomsman's job). Remember to have the flowers for the bridal party delivered to your home well before the photographer is due to arrive.

If the wedding is to be held some hours after the flowers must be collected you will need to ensure they are kept fresh with constant spraying. Florists should pack the arrangements with distance in mind.

ALTERNATIVES TO FLOWERS

If you are getting married in very hot weather, if someone in the bridal party suffers from hay fever, if the wedding is a distance from a florist, or simply if you want something more lasting for your money, you may look for substitutes for bridal flowers.

Headgear can be made from pearls, ribbon, lace, feathers or artificial flowers, while the bride and her bridesmaids can carry evening bags or frilly parasols. A white prayer-book was a popular choice half a century ago. Or, if you want the last word in elegance, consider a bouquet of silk flowers.

If it's floral arrangements that are the problem and you want something in addition to potplants and greenery, you can decorate pew ends with bows, and transform the interior of a marquee with parachute lining and fairy lights.

READINGS

Good readings can contribute to the theatre of the occasion. For the wedding ceremony many couples choose a reading from the Bible, Kahlil Gibran or Shakespeare. You may find a suitable love poem, for example among the works of Elizabeth Barrett Browning.

Many religious celebrants are happy for you to include a reading that isn't from the Bible; or, you can still have a religious reading if yours is a civil ceremony. If certain readings or poems have special meaning for you both, by all means arrange for them to be included in the ceremony. And if you want to have a reading at the reception, why not?

When you've decided all this, select readers who will be clearly heard, and who will practise beforehand, whether they are naturally good readers or not: a hesitant reading can have the company squirming, while a polished one can make the day.

MUSIC

Music can be a wonderful mood-setter both during the ceremony and at the reception. It can also be unmemorable or a disaster. There is plenty of suitable music available and what you choose will depend on your style of wedding (for a selection see Appendix 3).

Find out the rules

If you are having a religious ceremony keep in mind that there may be rules about what music is permitted. Check your music list with the officiating minister.

If you are holding your wedding ceremony in a public park it is best to check with the local council about what is permitted – some authorities do allow musicians in moderation, quartets rather than a big band sound; by others you will be limited to quiet taped music. For music at a registry office see p. 24.

When to play it

For church weddings it is usual to have music while the bride walks down the aisle, while the register is being signed, and while the bridal party and guests leave the church. (This general pattern may also be appropriate for a civil ceremony.) Beyond this, each denomination tends to follow its own pattern and you will need to discuss details with the officiating minister. For non-Christian religious weddings the requirements may be different again.

What kind of music?

Familiar choices for church ceremonies are Mendelssohn's 'Wedding March', Schubert's 'Ave Maria' or Clarke's 'Trumpet Voluntary'. Or you may want to walk down the aisle to 'Here Comes the Bride' (Wagner's *Lohengrin*).

The music at the church or wedding venue may be played by an organist, or you may organise orchestral instruments, a piano or a guitar. Popular music is sometimes appropriate. Songs or hymns may be sung by a soloist, a choir, or the assembled company (include the words in the service book or programme). Your exit may even be accompanied by the sound of bagpipes.

At the reception, once again your music should be what you like, and you will probably want to relate it to the style of your wedding. A string quartet is a popular choice. Background music (for example soft jazz) may be suitable for some weddings, while a mobile disco is probably appropriate if guests want to dance into the late hours. If you are having a reception at home consider taped music, or a disc jockey for dancing.

Whatever you select, the music should strike a happy balance for the age groups, and it should not be so overpowering that it prevents conversation.

Listen to it first!

Some reception centres provide an in-house band, but it is wise to check what type of music they play and watch them in action if you want to avoid a three-piece band serenading guests at their tables, or a disc jockey whose star turn includes a dance routine!

Once again, the key to success is to plan each small detail: you should listen, well in advance, to all the music you are likely to hear on the day.

PHOTOGRAPHS AND VIDEOS

As photographs can be a delightful record of the day, and also expensive (see p. 39), you need to be confident that your photographer will produce the goods.

Proper communication is vital. Think about what pictures you want. Do you want colour pictures, black and white, or a combination of both? Which are the priority shots? Posed or candid? Then write down what you want and give a copy to the photographer.

Candid shots are good for capturing the mood of the day, but you may want some set-up shots as well; the usual ones are the signing of the register, the cutting of the cake, the wedding party (with and without parents and immediate family), and the bride and groom alone. You will have to ask specifically for these shots. It's an obvious point, but often forgotten.

Remember that some ministers do not allow photography in the church (the signing of the register is usually an exception), while others don't allow photographers in the sanctuary, but don't mind them further back. Other celebrants, including civil celebrants, may make similar rules. Find out before you organise details with your photographer.

You should also have a clear idea of where you want post-ceremony photographs taken. Keep in mind that if a location is an obvious choice for you (perhaps the local gardens) it may also be the choice for other wedding parties – and you can expect queues.

Choosing your photographer

Here are some hints to help you make the right choice.

- If you have chosen a large **studio**, find out who your photographer will be.
- Examine a **sample album**. Make sure that the pictures are of one wedding, and not a collection of the photographer's best work. Are the photographs taken at the same time of day as your wedding, and in a similar setting?
- Scrutinise the **quality** of the prints. Can anything be done to improve the shots that don't make the grade?
- Discover exactly what the **fees** include. Will the photographer take the time for formal pictures before the ceremony, and stay until the end of the reception? Does the price include a specific number of photos? Can you keep your negatives and proofs? Are there hidden costs? Get the facts in writing before you commit yourselves.
- Inquire about **delivery** time. Make sure it is reasonable for both the proofs and the album: some photographers keep their clients waiting a year for their album, while others set a date by which clients must make their choice of proofs to be printed.
- Establish a **rapport** with your photographer. Exchange ideas about what you envisage for your wedding photographs. It's an important day, and worth recording to your taste.

Video etiquette

Videos have become increasingly popular at weddings and while the end result may be pleasing they do have drawbacks.

Looming lenses can be intrusive to guests and celebrants alike, and many couples will not want their every gesture recorded. Of course a video does have an advantage: it enables friends who were unable to attend to see some of your wedding.

A good compromise may be to videotape only certain parts of the ceremony and the reception, for example the arrival and departure at the wedding venues, the signing of the register, and guests during the early part of the reception.

And remember – not all wedding venues allow a video camera to be operated during the ceremony. Check ahead.

THE WEDDING CAKE

Traditionally the cake is a two- or three-tiered rich fruit cake, iced with almond and fondant icing, and appropriately decorated. The first tier is sliced and distributed at the reception by the bridesmaids, the second is kept for the first anniversary, and the final one is eaten at the christening of the first child.

What kind?

While the wedding cake remains an important focus at most weddings it may be any shape or form you fancy. Many couples choose a decorated sponge cake or the French-style croquembouche, an elaborate cone-shaped confection made of cream-filled pastry puffs and held together with toffee.

The advantage of the croquembouche is that it doubles as a dessert for the guests; the disadvantages are that it doesn't lend itself to the cake-cutting ritual, and doesn't keep. Think twice if your wedding day is likely to be very hot: on one memorable occasion a large croquembouche collapsed bit by bit around the bride as she made her speech, and had to be scraped up from the carpet by a procession of waiters!

Cutting it with style
Make sure that there *is* a knife: having to send out to the kitchen will spoil the moment. If you can beg or borrow an antique silver knife, or a military sword, yours will be cake-cutting with a difference. For further dash, tie a satin ribbon to the handle of the knife.

Kitchen cunning
Some people have a cake for show and another already sliced (and perhaps packaged) in the kitchen. This is especially appropriate if you are having many guests, as it saves having an awkwardly large cake, a certain amount of expense (the 'kitchen' cake need not be so elaborately decorated), and a frantic cutting-up chore.

Keeping your cake
Despite the custom of keeping wedding cake, this is not a practice recommended by cake shops. A rich fruit mixture containing alcohol is the best bet if you want a cake that keeps well. If you are determined to keep your cake, make sure you use an airtight container, but not a plastic one – or, better still, put it in the freezer.

12 THE RECEPTION

You've made it! The formalities are over and you are married. Now you can relax and revel in the occasion.

This chapter focuses on the traditional reception so often used as a model. Slavish adherence to it, however, is unlikely to produce a reception that is memorable for the right reasons! If certain traditions seem archaic to you, then ignore them; if the thought of the bridal waltz embarrasses you, don't do it; if you want to make a speech, go ahead. This is *your* day!

THE RECEIVING LINE

The traditional receiving line has an usher greeting guests and introducing them by name to the bride's parents (or whoever is hosting the wedding). The groom's parents are next in line, followed by the bridal couple, the chief bridesmaid, best man, and other attendants. If there is a big guest list it is best to keep the receiving line small – not all the attendants need be in it – otherwise you could be standing there for a very long time. As each person passes along the receiving line introductions are made and hands shaken. It is best to keep conversations short to keep the line moving.

Although the receiving line gives the bridal couple a chance to greet guests individually it does make for stiff introductions and can seem interminable. You may choose instead to mingle with your guests informally; but don't forget that it's important for you both to speak to every guest and thank them for their attendance, their good wishes, and their gifts if you can call them to mind.

THE SEATING

If you are having a sit-down reception the focus of the seating plan should be on the bridal couple, who traditionally sit with the bridal party and both sets of parents. If you are having long tables it is customary to seat only one side of the bridal table, so that the party faces the company; and you may like to consider a platform. If you are having round tables make sure that you are seated in the middle of the room.

The traditional bridal table is arranged in the following order (from left, facing table): bride's parents, bridesmaid, grooms-man, chief bridesmaid, groom, bride, best man, bridesmaid, groomsman, groom's parents. Some religions dictate the seating arrangements; for example at a Jewish reception the bridal couple sit with their parents, close relatives and the rabbi.

Often lack of space demands that parents sit at the second table rather than the bridal table. If your parents are divorced they may find it more comfortable to host separate tables; similarly, if the two sets of parents are not close they may be placed at different tables, perhaps adjoining ones. If the celebrant is attending it is customary for him or her to be seated with the parents of the bride.

Pageboys and flowergirls need not be seated at the bridal table and may be best placed at their own table, or with parents. Judge this by their age, their temperament, or play it by ear; some small attendants will feel rejected if they're not sitting with the bridal party, while for others it will be too much of an effort.

For the remainder of your guests aim for a happy mix: sit people with similar interests together, and try to ensure that each table has a good talker who will keep the conversation flowing. While it is not necessary to alternate the sexes, it may help to have tables evenly divided if you are having dancing.

Whatever you decide, remember that a seating plan placed at the entrance of the dining room will direct guests to their tables quickly and easily. Also have a contingency plan for guests who weren't expected to turn up, or have somehow been left off the list of acceptances. It *has* happened!

Guests are usually seated first and stand when the bridal couple is announced. The bride and groom should be served first, followed by the rest of the bridal table and the tables of the parents.

FORMALITIES

If yours is a religious wedding it may be customary to have religious ceremonies, prayers or blessings at the reception; for example at a Christian wedding grace may be said before the reception meal. If you don't know exactly what is done you should consult the officiating minister, who is likely to lead the religious ceremonies if he or she is attending the reception. At a Christian wedding the officiating minister is usually asked to say grace, but if he or she is not attending the reception anyone may say it.

Toasts

For a formal wedding reception there is a traditional pattern of toasts and replies, which may include the following in the order listed.

- **The loyal toast** (to the British monarch), proposed by the MC or the bride's father, without a speech. Guests are not supposed to smoke until after this.
- **Toast to the bridal couple**, proposed by a friend of the bride's family after a speech providing some thoughts on the occasion of the marriage.
- **Response by the groom on behalf of the couple**, including some reflections on the marriage and thanks to all involved in the day, and concluding with a toast to the bridesmaids.
- **Response by the best man on behalf of the bridesmaids**. The best man usually congratulates the groom on his bride, recalls his acquaintance with the couple, and wishes them success in their future life.
- **Toast to the parents of the bride**, made at the conclusion of a speech by a relative or friend.
- **Response by the bride's father**.
- **Toast to the parents of the bridegroom**.
- **Response by the bridegroom's father**.
- **Reading of the telegrams** by the best man and a groomsman. Speeches are usually made at the end of the meal and before

coffee is served, but if there are several it is best to start earlier and group them between courses. The trend has been to limit the number of speeches: few guests want to listen to more than two or three, and the traditional approach has proved too sexist for many. The toast to the bridal couple and the response (by the groom *or* the bride, or both) are considered the most important.

Guidelines for speeches

Wedding-reception speeches can be witty and entertaining interludes, but all too easily become embarrassing and boring monologues. Here are some pointers: pass them on to your speechmakers.

- Plan in advance (the speech should have a beginning, a middle and an end), and practise.
- Keep it short and to the point.
- Avoid off-colour jokes and 'in' remarks.
- Speak slowly and clearly.
- Avoid clichés.
- Aim to entertain – leave it to others to sermonise.
- Vet the telegrams and edit out anything unsuitable.
- Stay sober!

The cake-cutting

This follows the reading of the telegrams. The cake is usually on a separate table. With the groom's hand over the bride's, photographs are taken and the couple cut the cake together as a symbol of their shared life in the future. It is then taken away to be cut up and eaten as dessert or distributed to guests by the bridesmaids.

The bridal waltz

This formality, which usually takes place after the reading of the telegrams at an evening wedding, is fast fading from custom. If you are not having dancing you would probably not even consider it. The traditional order for the waltz is as follows: the bride and groom dance alone (perhaps one turn of a biggish dance floor, or for the first song); the bride's father then dances with his daughter and the groom dances with the bride's mother. Next the groom's father dances with the bride, and the groom with his mother, while the bride's parents dance together; then the rest of the guests join in.

TAKING YOUR LEAVE

The celebration is over and now it's time for the bridal couple to leave. You may feel that you want to party on all night – that's fine, but let your intention be known to the older guests, who will consider it ill-mannered to leave before you.

Many brides stay in their wedding dress, but if you are planning to change into a going-away outfit your bridesmaid should be ready to slip away to help you. On your return, the MC can announce your imminent departure or the band may strike up a farewell tune.

Your family and guests may form a circle around you and sing 'For They Are Jolly Good Fellows' or 'Auld Lang Syne' while you say goodbye to each guest, the bride moving in one direction and the groom in the other. If there are a large number of guests you may modify this, saying goodbye to your parents individually and giving the rest of the guests a wave at the door.

As a final gesture a bride may toss her bouquet over her shoulder to the single young women in the crowd (the one who catches it is supposed to be the next bride). A bride may also throw her garter (taken off by the groom) to the single young men. An old shoe (for luck) may be tied to the couple's car.

13 AFTER THE WEDDING

You've driven away. This should be the time to relax, gather your thoughts and begin to enjoy your time together as a married couple. But has your planning made this possible?

THE WEDDING NIGHT

Many couples choose to spend their wedding night at a hotel. If you are on a tight budget, however, and particularly if you are having an evening reception, consider whether the outlay of at least $150 is worth the short time you will spend there. You may plan to use the hotel room for 'partying on' after the reception – but before inviting revellers back to the room remember you will already have been on the go for many hours and are likely to feel emotionally and physically exhausted!

You may also feel hungry: it is likely that you've both been too busy doing the rounds of friends and family to sit down and eat at the reception. Consider ordering supper – perhaps with champagne – to be in your room on arrival, or, if you are going home, stock up your fridge with a midnight feast.

THE HONEYMOON

Traditionally the honeymoon destination has been the groom's secret. While this is a nice idea it can be fraught with problems. One friend was whisked off to an anxious time in Thailand: she had had none of the recommended vaccinations. If the location is to be kept a secret, perhaps the groom should let drop how long you will be going for, what to pack, what medical precautions to take, and whether you will need your passport.

When you are deciding where to go for your honeymoon keep your budget firmly in mind; don't start off with a debt. A weekend in the country or a week at the beach can be just as enjoyable as a luxurious jaunt in the Mediterranean.

DELAYING YOUR DEPARTURE

Although it may be seen as being unromantic, it may make good sense to organise your honeymoon departure date for a couple of days after the wedding: this takes the heat out of the pre-wedding week, allows you to catch up with people who have travelled a long way to the wedding, and gives you a chance to organise anything you've been forced to neglect. You may even be around to do the cleaning up!

WHEN YOU'VE GONE

So you've flown away on your honeymoon. Who returns the hired suits, takes down the marquee, and preserves the bouquet? This is the real test of your planning.

Returning hired suits
Returning hired suits should be the responsibility of a groomsman. He will also be able to collect the refund on the hire and to distribute the money to other attendants.

Dismantling the marquee
The marquee will be dismantled by the hire company, probably on the next working day. This will be automatic. But ask someone to oversee this, checking off what is being returned against the list made when the items arrived (see Chapter 3), and keeping the list in case of any discrepancy.

Returning hired crockery and cutlery
Organise with whoever is doing the cleaning up to tick off each item as it is washed, dried and packed away. Ensure that someone has been given the job of returning all hired items!

Returning borrowed bits and pieces
As above. Once back from your honeymoon, write a thank-you letter to each person who lent plants, vases, and so on.

Preserving the bouquet
If you want to preserve the bridal bouquet, here's how to do it. Place it in a cardboard box and completely cover it with borax or silica gel (available at chemists or hardware stores). This will dry it out. How long it takes will depend on the size of the bouquet. If you don't have time to do this before you leave on your honeymoon, ask someone else to do it and give them the necessary ingredients.

Minding the house
Plants need to be watered, letterboxes cleared, and perhaps the garden weeded. A friendly neighbour may be the best person to do this. Don't forget to cancel papers, and to notify the local police station or Neighbourhood Watch of your absence.

Developing the photographs
If you're not using a commercial photographer and you're intending to be away for some time, you'll need to appoint someone to get your films developed. As it can be an expensive process, cost it, and provide the money in advance.

CHANGING YOUR NAME

This may be a big step for a woman who is worried about losing her identity, and the couple should discuss the issue well before the wedding day. If it's not clear-cut, you may consider using your maiden name at work and your husband's name socially.

Some couples will find it more satisfactory to adopt both their surnames hyphenated; that is, Judith Pearson and Bill Smith become Judith and Bill Pearson-Smith.

It is an easy matter for a woman to adopt her married name legally. Simply take your marriage certificate to places where your maiden name is registered – the bank, tax department, Medicare, and your medical clinic.

UPDATING YOUR WILLS

As a marriage invalidates any existing wills you should consider visiting a solicitor together to draw up new ones that will become valid as soon as you are married.

Appendix 1
WEDDING TIMETABLE

THREE TO SIX MONTHS AHEAD

- Announce engagement (publicly through the newspaper, by note or telephone).
- Choose and buy engagement ring.
- Select attendants.
- Hold engagement party. Consider hosting a lunch or dinner for both families to meet.
- Record engagement presents as they arrive and send thank-you notes.
- Compile guest list and prepare a preliminary wedding budget.
- Check availability of church, wedding venue, registry office.
- Book reception centre.
- Book caterers (if required).
- Decide on style and fabric for bride's and bridesmaids' dresses. If being made, organise bookings with dressmaker.
- Book the hiring of suits for best man and groomsmen.
- Decide on wording of invitation, and place order with stationers.

SIX TO TEN WEEKS AHEAD

- Finalise guest list.
- Work out ceremony with minister or celebrant. Select readings and invite those you wish to read them.
- Organise music for the ceremony and prepare service and/or hymn sheets.
- Order remaining printed stationery – place cards, cake bags, table napkins, and so on.
- Work out detailed menu with caterers.
- Organise wedding gift list.
- Organise honeymoon and book hotel for wedding night.
- Renew passport if going on an overseas honeymoon.
- Have first fitting of wedding dress.
- Organise wedding cake.
- Book photographer.
- Obtain documentation from marriage celebrant.
- Select your MC, and ask him or her to perform that duty at your wedding.
- Organise accommodation for guests who will have to travel a long way to your wedding.
- Send invitations eight weeks before the wedding day.

FOUR TO SIX WEEKS AHEAD

- Book trial run with hairdresser.
- Record gifts as they arrive and send thank-you notes.
- Arrange further dress fittings for bride and bridesmaids.
- Buy bride's and bridesmaids' shoes.
- Meet photographer to discuss what will be required on the day.
- Organise practice ceremony.
- Book makeup artist and hairdresser for wedding day.
- Select and order floral arrangements and flowers for the bridal party.
- Confirm hire cars.
- Have necessary vaccinations if going on an overseas honeymoon.
- Obtain necessary visas if going on an overseas honeymoon.

FINAL TWO WEEKS

- Pick up rings.
- Finalise guest list with reception venue and caterers.
- Work out seating arrangements.
- Make final check of menu and wine list.
- Organise gift table at reception venue.
- Pre-wedding functions should be held in these weeks.
- Pick up bride's and bridesmaids' dresses after final fitting.
- Have practice ceremony.
- Final run-through with hairdresser.

- Buy presents for attendants.
- Organise someone to look after your house and garden while you're on your honeymoon.
- Book a security guard (if required) if you are holding the reception privately.
- Begin honeymoon packing.

DAY BEFORE

- Organise for going-away outfit (if wearing one) to be sent to reception venue.
- Finalise honeymoon packing.
- Organise flowers for the church and/or reception venue to be delivered.
- Make final check of seating arrangements, taking into account last-minute additions or deletions.

ON THE DAY

- Have bridal party flowers delivered to relevant addresses.
- Hair, makeup and nails for bride and bridesmaids.
- Photography at bride's home.
- Cars arrive.
- Congratulations – you've made it!

Appendix 2
REGISTRIES OF BIRTHS, DEATHS AND MARRIAGES

ACT
Birth, Death and Marriage Registry
GPO Box 788
Canberrra 2601
(02) 6207 0460

New South Wales
Registry of Births, Deaths and Marriages
GPO Box 30
Sydney 2001
1300 655 236

Northern Territory
Registry of Births, Deaths and Marriages
PO Box 3021
Darwin 0801
(08) 8999 6119

Queensland
Registry of Births, Deaths and Marriages
PO Box 188

Brisbane 4002
(07) 3247 9202

South Australia
Births, Deaths and Marriages Division
GPO Box 1351
Adelaide 5001
(08) 8204 9599

Tasmania
Registry of Births, Deaths and Marriages
GPO Box 198
Hobart 7001
(03) 6233 3793

Victoria
Registry of Births, Deaths and Marriages
PO Box 4332
Melbourne 3001
(03) 9603 5888

Western Australia
Registry of Births, Deaths and Marriages
PO Box 7720
Perth 6850
(08) 9264 1555

Appendix 3
MUSIC FOR THE CEREMONY

Bach	'Ave Maria'
Beethoven	'Song of Joy'
Brahms	'Waltz in A Flat'
Clarke	'Trumpet Voluntary'
Handel	'Arrival of the Queen of Sheeba'
Malotte	'The Lord's Prayer'
Mendelssohn	'Wedding March'
Parry	'Bridal March'
Schubert	'Ave Maria'
Wagner	'Bridal March' from *Lohengrin* ('Here Comes the Bride')

Appendix 4
FLORAL SUGGESTIONS

While many of the flowers mentioned below may not be suitable for bouquets, this list can be used as a guideline to give an idea and suggestions for flowers for the wedding venue and the reception venue.

Consider using Australian wildflowers. Flannel flowers, listed below, make a delicate bridal bouquet while showy blooms such as waratahs and leucodendron make magnificent displays.

WHITE

Spring

Agapanthus	Chrysanthemum	Gladiolus
Amaryllis	Crocus	Gloxinia
Anemone	Daffodil	Gypsophila
Apple blossom	Daisy	Hyacinth
Azalea	Delphinium	Iberis
Calla lily	Dianthus	Iris
Camellia	Flannel flower	Jasmine
Carnation	Freesia	Jonquil
Cherry blossom	Gardenia	Leucojum
Lilac	Ranunculus	Stock

Lily-of-the-valley
Lupin
Magnolia
Muscari
Primula

Rhododendron
Rose
Scilla
Snapdragon
Statice

Sweet pea
Tulip
Verbena

Summer

African daisy
Agapanthus
Amaryllis
Anthurium
Aster
Brachycome
Calla lily
Canna
Carnation
Chrysanthemum
Cornflower
Cosmos
Crocus
Daisy

Delphinium
Dianthus
Digitalis
Frangipani
Gardenia
Gladiolus
Gloxinia
Gypsophila
Hydrangea
Iris
Lilac
Lilium
Luneria
Lupin

Lychnis
Nierembergia
Orchid
Phlox
Rose
Snapdragon
Statice
Stock
Strawflower
Sweet pea
Verbena
Zinnia

Autumn

Aster
Azalea
Calla lily
Carnation
Gladiolus

Cosmos
Crocus
Daffodil
Daisy
Jonquil

Dianthus
Digitalis
Frangipani
Freesia
Rose

Gypsophila
Hyacinth
Iris

Lily-of-the-valley
Orchid
Primula

Tulip
Zinnia

Winter

Azalea
Camellia
Carnation
Chrysanthemum
Daffodil
Daisy
Delphinium

Freesia
Gladiolus
Gypsophila
Hyacinth
Iris
Jonquil
Lily-of-the-valley

Luneria
Lychnis
Orchid
Primula
Ranunculus
Rose
Tulip

YELLOW

Spring

Broom
Buttercup
Calceolaria
Calendula
Calla lily
Canna
Carnation
Celosia
Cheiranthus
Chrysanthemum
Poppy

Crocus
Daffodil
Daisy
Day lily
Digitalis
Freesia
Gazania
Gerbera
Geum
Gladiolus
Rose

Hollyhock
Honeysuckle
Hypericum
Iris
Ixia
Jonquil
Lupin
Orchid
Pansy
Polyanthus
Stock

| Ranunculus | Snapdragon | Tulip |
| Rhododendron | Statice | |

Summer

African daisy	Digitalis	Orchid
Calceolaria	Frangipani	Pansy
Calendula	Freesia	Poppy
Calla lily	Gazania	Ranunculus
Canna	Gerbera	Rose
Carnation	Geum	Snapdragon
Celosia	Gladiolus	Statice
Cheiranthus	Hibiscus	Stock
Chrysanthemum	Hollyhock	Strawflower
Crocus	Iris	Pansy
Dahlia	Lupin	Zinnia
Day lily	Marigold	

Autumn

African daisy	Dahlia	Marigold
Calceolaria	Daisy	Orchid
Calla lily	Gerbera	Poppy
Carnation	Hibiscus	Rose
Chrysanthemum	Iris	Zinnia
Daffodil	Lupin	

Winter

| Azalea | Canna | Chrysanthemum |
| Calendula | Carnation | Daffodil |

Dahlia
Freesia
Gladiolus
Hollyhock

Jonquil
Lupin
Orchid
Ranunculus

Rose
Tulip

BLUE/MAUVE/PURPLE

Spring

Achimenes
Agapanthus
Ageratum
Anemone
Brachycome
Cineraria
Cornflower
Day lily
Delphinium
Digitalis
Forget-me-not
Freesia

Gentian
Hollyhock
Hyacinth
Iris
Larkspur
Lavender
Lilac
Luneria
Magnolia
Muscari
Orchid
Penstemon

Polyanthus
Primula
Rhododendron
Schizanthus
Scilla
Statice
Sweet pea
Torenia
Viola
Zinnia

Summer

Achimenes
Agapanthus
Ageratum
Anclusa
Anemone
Iris

Aster
Brachycome
Cornflower
Day lily
Delphinium
Nigella

Digitalis
Freesia
Gloxinia
Hyacinth
Hydrangea
Scilla

Lavender
Linaria
Luneria
Lupin
Nierembergia

Orchid
Penstemon
Phlox
Plumbago
Schizanthus

Statice
Sweet pea
Sweet William
Torenia
Verbena

Autumn

Achimenes
Anchusa
Aster
Day lily
Delphinium

Freesia
Hollyhock
Hydrangea
Iris
Lavender

Orchid
Statice
Viola
Zinnia

Winter

Anemone
Chinese
  forget-me-not
Cornflower
Digitalis

Freesia
Gloxinia
Hyacinth
Iris
Lavender

Lupin
Primula
Stock
Viola

PINK

Spring

Achimenes
Ageratum
Amaryllis
Camellia

Anemone
Apple blossom
Armeria
English daisy

Azalea
Brachycome
Calla lily
Primula

Canna
Carnation
Cherry blossom
Chrysanthemum
Cineraria
Clematis
Coral bells
Cornflower
Crocus
Dahlia
Delphinium
Dianthus

Freesia
Gladiolus
Gloxinia
Hyacinth
Hollyhock
Iris
Ixia
Larkspur
Lilium
Lupin
Penstemon
Poppy

Ranunculus
Rose
Schizanthus
Snapdragon
Statice
Stock
Sweet pea
Verbena
Water lily
Watsonia

Summer

Achimenes
Ageratum
Amaryllis
Anemone
Armeria
Aster
Brachycome
Calla lily
Camellia
Canna
Carnation
Chrysanthemum
Clematis
Snapdragon

Coral bells
Cornflower
Cosmos
Crocus
Dahlia
Delphinium
Dianthus
English daisy
Freesia
Gladiolus
Gloxinia
Godetia
Hollyhock
Strawflower

Hyacinth
Hydrangea
Jasmine
Lilium
Linaria
Lupin
Penstemon
Peony
Phlox
Poppy
Ranunculus
Rose
Schizanthus
Verbena

Statice   Sweet pea   Zinnia
Stock   Tiger lily

Autumn
Achimenes   Dahlia   Ranunculus
Armeria   Delphinium   Rose
Aster   Gladiolus   Statice
Canna   Hyacinth   Zinnia
Carnation   Lilium
Coral bells   Poppy

Winter
Amaryllis   Dahlia   Poppy
Azalea   Freesia   Ranunculus
Calla lily   Hollyhock   Rose
Carnation   Iris   Statice
Chrysanthemum   Lupin
Cornflower   Penstemon

Appendix 5
GIFT SUGGESTIONS

The following may help you draw up a list for placement in a department store, with a parent or an attendant.

KITCHEN

blender
casserole dishes
chopping block
coffee percolator
coffee grinder
cookery books
crockery (everyday)
cutlery (everyday)
deep freeze
electric kettle or jug
electric wok
food processor
freezer storage bowls
frying pan
garlic press
glasses (everyday)
jugs

juice extractor
microwave oven
mixing bowls
pastry board and cutters
picnic set
place mats (everyday)
pressure cooker
quiche dish
salad bowl and servers
sandwich maker
saucepans
spice rack
storage jars
tablecloth, table napkins
  (everyday)
teapot
toaster

DINING

butter dish and knife
candlesticks
carving set
cheese platter
coffee pot
coffee cups
condiment set
dessert dishes
dinner set
drink coasters
egg cups
fish knives and forks
fruit bowl
glasses (wine, champagne, sherry, and so on)
gravy boat
ice bucket
jam pot and spoon
ladle
nutcracker
placemats
salt and pepper mills
silver cutlery
serving platters
soup tureen and bowls
steak knives
table cloth, table napkins
vases
water-jug and glasses
wine
wine decanter
wine storage unit

BEDROOM

bed
bedside tables
bedspread
blankets
chest of drawers
clock radio
doona
doona cover and valance
eiderdown
electric blanket
lamps
mirror
pillows and pillowcases
reading lamps
sheets

BATHROOM

bath mats
bath towels and sheets
bathroom scales
decorative storage jars
facecloths

guest towels
hand towels
linen basket
mirror
first aid kit

APPLIANCES

air conditioner
CD player
clock
heater
iron
modem

radio
television
tumble dryer
vacuum cleaner
video
washing machine

GARDEN AND OUTDOORS

barbecue and tools
citronella candles
clothesline
compost bin
garden lights
garden tools
garden umbrella
gardening books

hose
lawnmower
planter pots
sprinkler system
stepladder
table and chairs
wheelbarrow

GENERAL

books

camera

chairs

coffee table

cushions

gift voucher

lamps

luggage

photo frames

pictures and paintings

rug

subscription

wastepaper baskets

Appendix 6
WEDDING ANNIVERSARIES

First	paper/clocks
Second	cotton/china
Third	leather/crystal
Fourth	books/appliances
Fifth	wood/silverware
Sixth	sugar/iron
Seventh	wool/table sets
Eighth	bronze/linen
Ninth	pottery/leather
Tenth	tin/diamonds
Eleventh	steel/jewellery
Twelfth	silk/pearls
Thirteenth	lace/textiles
Fifteenth	crystal/watches
Twentieth	china/platinum
Twenty-fifth	silver
Thirtieth	pearls
Fortieth	rubies
Forty-fifth	sapphires
Fiftieth	gold
Fifty-fifth	emeralds
Sixtieth	diamonds

Appendix 7
THE WEDDING BOOK STARTER

The following forms can be photocopied and inserted in a folder or stuck into an exercise book to help you keep track of gifts received and thank-you letters sent. Keep separate lists for engagement and wedding gifts, and make sure that you have your wedding book handy whenever you open parcels. Remembering to record all the details will mean no heartache over lost cards!

From	Gift	Date received	Letter sent

From	Gift	Date received	Letter sent